ALIENS ON EARTH!

BY JOSHUA STRICKLAND

Illustrated by Frank Aloise
With an introduction by Erich von Däniken

Grosset & Dunlap
A Filmways Company
Publishers • New York

Acknowledgments

Pictures on pages 10, 11, 12, 13, 14, 15, 16, and 74 adapted from *Flying Saucer Review*.

Pictures on pages 8, 26, 27, 28, 30, and 89 adapted from *Document 96*, by Frank Martin Chase, published by Saucerian Press, Inc., Clarksburg, West Virginia.

Tables on pages 58, 59, 60, 61, 62, and 63 from *Flying Saucer Review*, Vol. 19, No. 3, pages 19–22.

Photographs on pages 17, 29, 49, 64, 69, and 71 courtesy of UPI.

Pictures on pages 38, 40, 41, 42, 43, 44, 45, 46, 47, and 48 adapted from United States Air Force *Project Blue Book, Number 14*.

Pictures on pages 50, 53, 55, and 56 from a paper presented by Hayden C. Hewes at the 2nd Midwest UFO Conference in 1971.

Copyright © 1977 by Joshua Strickland
Introduction Copyright © 1977 by Erich von Däniken
All rights reserved
Library of Congress Catalog Card Number: 77-71532
ISBN: 0-448-12898-5 (Trade Edition)
ISBN: 0-448-13416-0 (Library Edition)
Published simultaneously in Canada
Printed in the United States of America

Table of Contents

	Introduction	7
1.	The Beings—Eyewitness Reports	9
2.	From Wolf 424?	31
3.	The Ships—Eyewitness Reports	39
4.	The Anatomy of the Strangers	51
5.	Horses, Hattocks, and Kugelblitzes	65
6.	'h' and the End of the Ether	77
7.	What Are They?	83
	Notes	91
	Bibliography	92
	Index	93

Introduction
A letter to the gentleman "from the other star"

Dear Other-Star-Being:

The chance that you will read this letter equals zero. The chances that you will learn of its contents are small, but not zero. You have long been familiar with the possibility of sending conscious concepts through conscious energies safely across the widest distances and over all impediments. You and your colleagues—to whom I send my cordial greetings—probably have applied such methods successfully from time immemorial. Here, we still plod along. Too many terrestrial scholars are still in a childhood stage of development, cutting their first teeth. You might not believe that.

Accordingly, any questions I ask, as an intuitive product of your heritage, might impress you as foolish and naïve. But who would know better than you, my friend, that our recent human history limps hopefully behind your knowledge, which is milleniums older. It would be fantastic if once again you would lend us a helping hand in the course of a forthcoming visit. When did you and your team of astronauts visit our planet most recently? And where did you deposit the instruments and the transmitter you left behind? For reasons I can well understand, our archeologists always dig in the wrong places. I have my own ideas on the subject, but a hint from you would be useful—and may save you a troublesome voyage down to earth.

For some time now, we too have been building spaceships. These fire-spitting monsters will probably evoke only a gentle headshake from you, since they are still in a primitive stage. However—and you will agree, I am sure—we had to start somewhere, sometime. How long, with how many scientists, and with what financial and energy-powered means have your people worked in the field of space-travel development? Here on earth we seem to lose our work drives after but a few seconds (speaking in terms of development history). Don't you agree that this is very stupid? And shortsighted?

What are your energy sources? And how is your supply holding out? Here our oil and coal resources are dwindling. You will not believe it, but we still use these priceless raw materials for heating. Please do not smile.

I am convinced that for a long time you have used other energies. And I am also convinced that you found these new energy sources at the same time that you conducted space exploration. Here, however, we put the cart before the horse: we want to see the fruits of space exploration no later than one year after that exploration begins. You have been clever and have unending staying power. You know our small planet Earth. Can you imagine that on this planet hundreds of millions suffer from hunger? Because they happily go on procreating ever-more innocent beings. Supposedly superclever men dispute endlessly on how the peoples of the earth can survive diminishing resources and insufficient food supplies. They do not realize that their one chance of salvation is space exploration, through which they would find a new technology that would eliminate such large-scale suffering. A new visit from you would be enlightening in this respect too!

Here uncounted books are published. They do not always contain anything new. Mostly old ideas are polished and age-old wisdoms are served up again. But this is not true of one new work. A new, intelligent book is now presented to mankind: *Aliens on Earth!* I wish I could take you the first copy via a ship traveling at the speed of light. You would enjoy it!

Yours with interstellar greetings,

Erich von Däniken
April, 1977

1

The Beings–Eyewitness Reports

◆ ◆ ◆ ◆ ◆ ◆ ◆ ◆ ◆ ◆ ◆ ◆ ◆ ◆ ◆ ◆ ◆

Over the past twenty-five years, there have been more than three hundred reports from various parts of the world of the presence of strange manlike beings, often small in size. Frequently, they have been seen near unusual contraptions—entering or leaving them, working on them, or collecting things in their vicinity. The contraptions fly by some unknown method, often attaining great speeds and even vanishing into thin air.

Who are these beings? Are they products of overactive imaginations, or are they real? If real, where do they come from? Are they fellow denizens of our own planet who mostly keep hidden from view? Or are they from other worlds or places? Before we try to answer these questions, let us review a few of the sightings of the creatures.

Rosa Lotti was on her way to the local cemetery to lay flowers on the grave of her sister. It was early morning, in the province of Arrezo, Italy, and Signora Lotti was taking a shortcut through the woods, walking barefoot and holding her stockings and shoes in her hands along with the flowers. Beneath some trees at the edge of a clearing she noticed a curious

---

The lone report of dwarfs seen aboard a craft in the air comes from a missionary school at Boaini, New Guinea. The small "men" seen on the deck while the machine hovered 400 feet overhead responded with waves when waved to. Several times the creatures bent over something on the deck, and a bright-blue narrow beam of light would shoot skyward. There were a number of witnesses, including the school's director, Reverend William B. Gill. The craft was seen in the daytime and was estimated to be 30 to 40 feet in diameter. It was first witnessed on June 26, 1957, but returned on subsequent days.

Signora Lotti and the elves, near Cennina, Italy.

construction. It was about 6 feet high and 3 feet wide, shaped like a spindle and apparently covered with smooth, gleaming leather. Two little men, about 3 feet high, suddenly emerged from behind the spindle. They wore gray overalls that extended downward to cover their feet, short cloaks fastened to their shoulders, and doublets with shiny buttons.

Although they were the size of small children, their faces beneath their gray helmets were those of older men. Their short teeth protruded somewhat, like those of rabbits. They signaled Signora Lotti in a friendly fashion, meanwhile chatting to each other in what sounded like Chinese: "Liu, lai, loi, lau, loi, lai, liu."

The older-looking of the two men, she later reported, was more jolly, laughing a great deal. She was impressed by their eyes, which appeared to be full of intelligence. They snatched away the carnations Signora Lotti was carrying, and one of her black stockings. When she indicated her distress, the older dwarf returned two of her flowers, then wrapped the rest in the stocking and tossed them into an opening in the spindle.

Inside the spindle, Signora Lotti could see two small chairs, each with a porthole in front of it, and what looked like controls. When the older dwarf reached inside and removed some round white "packages," Signora Lotti ran away. Looking back several seconds later she could still see the dwarfs and their strange spindle.

◆ ◆ ◆ ◆ ◆ ◆

One Sunday afternoon, a Brazilian soldier named José Antonio da Silva, who was spending a quiet weekend fishing in a small lagoon about a hundred miles from his home, was kidnapped by three small men. His abductors, about 3 feet 8 inches tall, wore shining, light-colored garments with joints at the elbows and knees. Helmets came down to their shoulders, and from beneath them issued plastic hoses that led to small boxes on their backs.

The ship that carried da Silva away.

They stunned da Silva with a ray that was green in the middle and red on the outside, then carried him to a 9-foot-high spool-shaped machine. He was taken to a small compartment, about 6 by 6 by 6 feet, brightly illuminated with no apparent source of light, which just seemed to come out of the walls, floor, and ceiling. They put a helmet on José's head, closed the door, fastened his feet and his waist, and took off, manipulating the machine with levers and talking among themselves in gutteral tones with lots of "r" sounds.

After a trip, the craft landed and José was dragged outside, where he found himself in a large room being stared at by a dwarf with long red hair and a red beard that ended at his stomach. The dwarf had large, thick eyebrows, big green eyes, pale skin, a long pointed nose, large ears, and a

One of da Silva's dwarfs. He was the only observer (except possibly Villas Boas) who saw the same creature both with and without its "space suit."

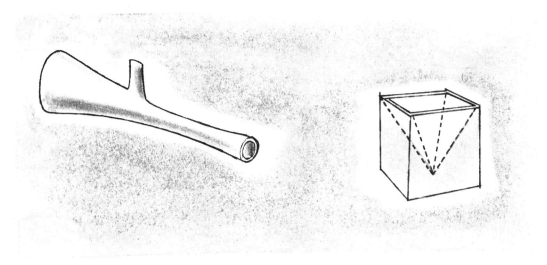

A dwarf's weapon, and the utensil from which da Silva drank.

mouth devoid of teeth. The room was as mysteriously illuminated as the inside of the "ship" and had, along one wall, a large painting of scenes of earth: houses, automobiles, and interesting animals (an elephant, a giraffe, and others). On a slab nearby lay four human corpses.

The beings carefully went through José's belongings, taking one of everything of which he had duplicates, but also keeping his military identification card, although he had only one copy. They gave him a green drink in a cube-shaped cup and, communicating with him by gestures and sketches, told him they wished him to return to earth to spy for them for three years. Afterwards they would fetch him for seven years of training, preparatory to an invasion.

Da Silva kept refusing and praying with his rosary beads until a vision of a handsome human figure appeared and gave him a secret message. The dwarfs then began quarreling with each other, placed the helmet back on the Brazilian's head, and, after another long journey, returned him to the edge of a stone quarry, 210 miles southeast of the lagoon where he had been seized. Although da Silva had dined only once, on the green liquid in the square cup, he was to find that four and a half days had passed.

A 3 foot high greenish man in a helmet and "space suit" was seen with what looked like a metal detector in the backyard of a Belgian's home late one night when its owner, M. Ivorde, got up to visit the outhouse. It had pointed ears and large luminous yellow eyes surrounded by green rims. When it lowered its eyelids, the face, deprived of the glow from the eyes, became invisible. When M. Ivorde shone a flashlight at it, the creature walked up a wall. Shortly afterwards, it flew off in a 15-foot-wide flying saucer.

How M. Ivorde's little man climbed the back wall.

M. Ivorde's little man departs.

◆ ◆ ◆ ◆ ◆ ◆

While hunting elk at the northern edge of Medicine Bow National Forest, a Wyoming oil driller named Carl Higdon was startled when a bullet he fired at one of the big animals slowly traveled just 50 feet from the barrel of his gun before falling to the ground. Then, in the shadows nearby, he noticed a 6 foot 2 inch "man" clad in a black, tight-fitting suit that resembled a diver's wet suit, clasped by a belt with a shining yellow six-pointed star. The creature was bowlegged, with a slanted head, hair that stood straight up, no chin, and one long finger in place of a hand. It pointed its "finger" at Higdon, and the hunter found himself in a small cubicle, lighted by a bright glow emanating from the walls, with two other "men" and five elk. Higdon was asked if he wanted to go with them,

The tall humanoid seen by Carl Higdon.

and agreed. He was strapped in, a helmet was placed on his head, and almost instantly he arrived at a "tall tower similar to the . . . Seattle space needle . . . (with) light so intense it hurt his eyes." The "men" explained that earth's light affected them in the same way, which was why they kept in the shade. They took Higdon back after explaining that their planet was "163,000 miles" from earth. Two and a half hours later Higdon was returned to his truck, which somehow had become mired in a swamp. He radioed for help and was rescued by friends five hours later.

At seven o'clock one November evening, the driver of a panel truck in West Virginia was forced to stop when a strange black vehicle shaped like a big kerosene lamp landed sideways on the road in front of him. The driver of the truck, Woodrow Derenberger, was accosted by a swarthy man with long dark hair combed straight back, who kept his arms crossed and his hands tucked into the armpits of his topcoat, beneath which could be seen a glistening green garment. The stranger, who was about 5 feet 10 inches tall, conversed with Derenberger by means of mental telepathy. While they "talked" the kerosene-lamp-shaped vehicle hovered in the air 50 feet above the ground and was seen by others in passing cars. On later occasions, the stranger, whose name was Mr. Indrid Cold, sent Derenberger mental messages, explaining that he was from the "planet Lanulos in the galaxy of Ganymede," a lovely place devoid of war, poverty, hunger, or misery.

Woodrow Derenberger holding a press conference the night after meeting Mr. Indrid Cold on Interstate Route 77. One can imagine that an interest in publicity would cause some people to invent stories of meeting strange beings. On the other hand, others passing Derenberger on Route 77 are said to have seen Mr. Cold and the strange machine in the sky.

At half past eight on the evening of August 21, 1879, Mrs. Mary McLoughlin, housekeeper to Archdeacon Cavanagh of Knock, a village in west Ireland, noticed a white light in a field as she passed the church on her way to visit a friend, Mrs. Beirne. As it was raining heavily, she did not stop to investigate. However, a short while later, while Mrs. McLoughlin and Mrs. Beirne were returning, they noticed three persons standing in a very bright light on the uncut field between them and the church. The central figure was Saint Mary, with Saint Joseph on her right and Saint John the Evangelist on her left. Soon sixteen other villagers had gathered before the apparitions, recognized because of their resemblance to religious paintings and sculptures.

The most striking part of the vision, all agreed when the matter was investigated by a church commission, was the very bright light that kept changing shape and color. Sometimes it lit up the sky above and beyond the church, then diminished and grew dim before swelling and becoming bright again, then becoming so bright that the gable of the church looked like a "wall of snow."

The three figures seen by all inside the light wore dazzling white silverlike garments. They stood in front of an altar with a large cross, before which lay, "face to the west," a young lamb. When one of the witnesses tried to embrace Saint Mary, her arms closed on air. She noticed, however, that even though rain was falling, the ground beneath the vision was dry.

The parish priest's explanation of the phenomenon was that it was caused by reflections from the stained-glass windows of the church, but tests showed that neither this nor a magic lantern could have produced what was seen. A number of miraculous cures were reported around Knock during the ensuing months.

On the 4th of July, 1950, Daniel Fry, a rocket technician at White Sands, New Mexico, was invited aboard a "flying saucer" he found sitting on the desert. He was taken on a quick trip to New York and back at an average speed of 8,000 miles an hour. He never saw his host, who claimed to be in a process of adapting to earth conditions.

Daniel Fry approaches the "flying saucer" at White Sands, New Mexico.

Antonio Villas Boas, a 5 foot 4 inch tall young Brazilian farmer who was plowing a field with a tractor in the middle of the night, was taken aboard an egg-shaped machine by four creatures, one of whom came up only to his shoulder. They escorted Antonio into a circular room illuminated by square lights set into the ceiling and around the tops of the walls. "I believe that this room," Antonio later reported, "was in the center of the machine for, in the middle of the room, there was a metal column running from ceiling to floor . . . [which] must have served to support the weight of the ceiling. The only furniture that I could see was a strangely shaped table that stood on one side of the room, surrounded by several backless swivel chairs." The little men were completely covered with tight-fitting gray coveralls and huge helmets that made their heads appear twice human size. The soles of their shoes were 3 inches thick and curled up in front. Conversing with what sounded like the barking and yelping of dogs, Antonio's abductors undressed him and washed him in some clear liquid and then took him to another room, where samples of blood were removed from each side of his chin by a tube that sucked it out through his skin. The only furniture in this small room was a sort of bed with a raised hump in the middle. As Villas Boas sat on it, smoke that issued from small holes in the walls made him sick and he had to vomit.

A doctor who examined Villas Boas afterwards, noted the strange circular bruises on his chin where the blood samples had been taken, and found him to exhibit symptoms of radiation sickness for several weeks.

◆ ◆ ◆ ◆ ◆ ◆

Mr. and Mrs. Barney Hill lost consciousness when they stopped their car to investigate a strange light that had been following them on a New Hampshire country road. Two and a half years later, under hypnosis, they recalled having been taken aboard a lens-shaped "ship" and subjected to "medical" examinations, which included sticking a needle into Mrs. Betty Hill's navel, examining Barney Hill's groin, and removing his false teeth. Betty Hill drew from memory a star chart she had seen inside the ship. An astronomical researcher later claimed to have identified the stars, among which were several that had not been discovered at the time of the Hills' abduction.

The creatures had large heads tapering down to tiny chins, slitlike mouths, and slanting eyes that went partway around the sides of their heads. This description is strangely like that of Antonio Villas Boas, although neither the Hills nor Villas Boas could have known of one another's experiences. It also tallies with that given by a Frenchman,

Helmeted creatures bathe Brazilian Antonio Villas Boas.

Maurice Masse, who, at five forty-five on the morning of July 1, 1965, saw a small oval-shaped machine, about the size of an automobile, standing on a center column surrounded by six legs in the middle of one of his lavender fields. For several days he and his father had noticed that lavender plants had been plucked from the field. When he saw two "small boys" near the machine, he assumed they were the culprits. As M. Masse approached, he saw that they were not boys at all, but creatures less than 4 feet tall, with pumpkinlike heads, high fleshy cheeks, large slanted eyes that extended around the sides of the face, slit mouths "without muscular lips," and pointed chins. When Masse got within 16 feet of them, one creature pointed a small tube at him and he was unable to move. They entered the machine, which took off and, at a distance of 20 yards, just disappeared.

On the night of September 4, 1964, a bow-and-arrow hunter in the mountains above Truckee, on the California-Nevada border, was separated from his two companions. He climbed a tree when he was approached by a strange white light, about 8 or 10 inches in diameter, that moved around and hovered motionless nearby in the air. Later, in the moonlight, he saw a "dome-shaped affair" about a quarter of a mile away, either on or near the ground. His tree was soon approached by three neckless creatures: two were about 5 feet 5 inches tall, clothed in a silvery-gray material that covered their heads. The third walked in a clumsy, noisy fashion, going through bushes instead of around them, had 3 inch red-orange eyes that glowed and flickered, and a rectangular mouth, as wide as the "head," that dropped open. The two hooded figures kept trying to climb the tree to get at the hunter. When they failed, the other creature, which the hunter assumed to be a robot, opened its mouth and belched puffs of white smoke or gas, which, when they reached the hunter, made him light-headed or unconscious, and nauseated when he awoke. This went on all night. Arrows that the hunter shot at the bug-eyed creature made a metallic sound when they struck. To keep his tormentors at bay, the hunter also tore off pieces of his clothing, lit them with matches, and dropped them on them. At dawn, another bug-eye joined the three creatures. The two "robots," facing each other, generated a large cloud of gas between their chests. When the hunter awoke in his tree, he was sick to his stomach and the creatures were gone.

Maurice Masse confronts strange creatures with pumpkinlike heads, standing beside an oval machine in his lavender field.

Terrifying night in the mountains. A hunter near Truckee is treed by weird visitors.

Shortly before two thirty in the morning on December 3, 1967, Patrolman Herbert Schirmer was taken aboard a 100 foot diameter craft, which he found sitting in a field near Ashland, Nebraska. The four aliens he encountered were between 4½ and 5 feet tall, with large chests and a muscular, wiry appearance. Their postures were rigid and their heads were thinner and longer than those of human beings, with slanting eyebrows above catlike eyes that gave them a slightly oriental appearance. Their noses were long and flat, and their lips were very thin, their mouths almost a slit. Their skin was whitish gray and they wore boots and silvery seamless coveralls with belts on which were small holsters. There were small antennae on their helmets.

Aliens in Nebraska take Patrolman Schirmer aboard their ship.

As we have seen, the creatures exhibit many different characteristics. Some have had glowing eyes, others glowing lights in their belts. Some have worn helmets with what appeared to be breathing apparatuses. Others have walked about as if they were comfortable in our atmosphere. When shot, some have fallen to the ground as if wounded, others have appeared to be unaffected. One Hopkinsville, Kentucky, goblin, dislodged from a roof by a bullet, floated to the ground and arose unharmed. Some have appeared peaceful, others have been mischievous,

The 3 to 4 foot figures seen on the deck of this craft when it landed in a cove of Steep Rock Lake, Ontario, moved slowly like robots "changing direction without turning their bodies." One wore a bright-red skull cap; the others' caps were blue. Metallic breastplates were fitted over their gray garments. When they noticed they were being watched, they drew in the hoses, cleared the deck, and took off. The ship was about 40 feet in diameter and 8 feet high. It was seen by a mining executive and his wife on July 2, 1950.

Gustave Gonzales and José Ponce, driving a truck in Petare, an outlying part of Caracas, Venezuela, found their way blocked by a glowing disklike object about 10 feet in diameter, which hovered 6 feet over the ground. When they got out to investigate, Gonzales was attacked by a hairy little creature with claws and glowing eyes. He grabbed it and found it weighed only about 45 pounds. It felt as if it were hollow and very hard beneath its fur. As it pushed Gonzales back, two other dwarfs jumped into the machine, carrying stones. Gonzales was temporarily blinded by a bright light. The machine then rose and flew away. A physician driving behind the truck witnessed the encounter. Two weeks later (December 10, 1954), several hundred miles southwest of Caracas, two boys came upon a glittering 10-foot machine flashing fiery light from its bottom, landing beside the Trans-Andean Highway near the country village of Chico. Four strong hairy dwarfs attacked the boys, who fought them off and got away.

When Marius DeWilde's dog started barking, DeWilde went outside his house to find that a large dark object had landed on nearby railroad tracks. As he approached the "ship," the Frenchman encountered two small manlike creatures in shiny helmets. Stunned by a dazzling beam of orange light, he watched as an opening appeared in the side of the object and it took off, roaring away into the night. Five deep indentations were found in the wood crossties and stone ballast where the machine had rested, from which French Air Force officials and police estimated that the weight of the object was 30 tons. (Quarouble, France, September 10, 1954.)

and some have used tubelike weapons with paralyzing rays, or emitted strange gases from their mouths that have had a similar effect. Witnesses have often reported that sightings of ships and their occupants were accompanied by strong feelings of alarm or its opposite, and that for several days afterward their eyes watered or they had headaches or other mysterious pains. A few have noted that wounds healed unaccountably quickly or that infections disappeared. One old Brazilian grew a third set of teeth after a visit by dwarfs.

Some creatures have talked the language of those who met them, whether it was English, French, Spanish, or Portuguese. Others have mouthed unearthly tongues with weird melodic or guttural sounds and have sought to communicate by sign language. Still others have employed mental telepathy. Often they volunteered information as to their origin, saying they came from Mars or Venus or Lanulos or another galaxy. In one instance, which shall now be examined in detail, they claimed, very precisely, to have come from the planetary system of a star just fourteen and a fraction light years from our sun.

Marius de Wilde and Kiki, the dog whose barking caused him to go out and see the machine and its little men.

2

From Wolf 424?

◆ ◆

In 1971, Gordon Creighton, one of the editors of the British publication *Flying Saucer Review*, received from a Spanish writer on UFO's, Señor Antonio Ribera, a report on, and examples of, communications with beings from another planet. The material dealt with denizens of the planet UMMO, of which Creighton had heard rumors for a number of years. As some of the papers were of a technical nature, it took Creighton a considerable time to translate them, with the result that the UMMO affair did not appear in English until 1974.

In his report to Creighton, Ribera explained that he had first heard of the UMMO communications in 1967, when a man from Barcelona who had read one of his "flying saucer" books told him that a friend of his, Don Enrique Villagrasa Novoa, a civil engineer, had been having lengthy telephone conversations with mysterious beings who also sent him written reports on technical subjects.

Subsequently, Ribera learned that about twenty persons in Spain, together with others in France, East Germany, Argentina, and a number of other countries, had also been receiving typewritten papers from the UMMO beings. The Spanish recipients included a well-known playwright, a lawyer, an official of the telegraph department known for his interest in life on other worlds, a young lady employed by the American embassy,

Unmatjera tribesmen watched these disks, about 40 feet in diameter and "a man and a half high," land in the desert in central Australia. A small manlike figure in a shiny suit, with either a large head or a helmet, emerged from the bottom of one of the two craft and entered the other. The two disks emitted a humming noise as they swiftly zoomed upward. (September, 1951.)

and so on. They were not, for reasons that the UMMITES would explain, leaders of their country.

The UMMITES claimed to have discovered earth in 1948, when they "picked up a faint signal with a frequency of 413.44 megacycles, which we were unable to decipher." Although the signal lasted only 6.8 minutes (2.2 UIW—the unit of UMMO time), it was sufficient for them to "identify, on galactic coordinates, the position of the solar system." The signal they picked up, the UMMITES were to learn after coming to earth, had been sent in Morse code. At the time, thinking that the dots and dashes were a binary code of the kind used in computers (dots, zeroes, dashes, ones), they had erroneously composed from them a "message," which gave the graph of a geometric figure they called a GAA, from which they had given our planet the name OOYAGAA (cold star of GAA).

"At 04 hours 17 minutes 03 seconds GMT on the terrestrial day of March 28, 1950," they wrote, "an OAWOLEA UEWA OEM (lenticular-shaped-spaceship) established contact for the first time in history with the lithosphere of earth.

"The landing took place in a particular area of the Department des Basses-Alpes (France), at a place some 8,000 meters distant from the town of La Javie.

"Six of my brethren led by OEOE 95, son of OEOE 91, and including two YIEE (women), remained behind on this OYAA (planet) as the first expedition (INAYUYISAA) from UMMO."

Creighton reports that "several of France's top students of the UFO phenomena" are familiar with strange events that took place in the vicinity of La Javie. The former owners of a miserable and dilapidated farm there, it was said, were found living in grand style on the French Riviera, their mouths sealed as to the source of their good fortune or the reason for their move.

After spending some time adapting to earth and learning its customs and languages, the UMMITES investigated the source of the 413.44 megacycle signals they had picked up in 1948, and learned that they had been broadcast by "a Norwegian ship on the latitude of Newfoundland, in the course of certain experiments . . . relating to the use of high frequencies in communication over great distances by ionospheric reflection. The signal was sent out between February 5 and 7, 1934."

The UMMITES claimed that it was not easy for them to identify for us the exact location of their sun (IUMMA), a star of small mass (OOYIA), due to slight errors in our astronomical tables. "We calculate," they wrote, "that the coordinates familiar to you that might establish the position of IUMMA would be:

Solid angle defined by

Right ascension 12 hours, 31 minutes, 14 seconds ± 2 min, 11 sec. Declination 9°18'7" ± 14'2"

"It so happens that very near the center of this probable stereo-angle . . . some of the tables drawn up by you indicate a star which you call WOLF 424."

The UMMITES state, however, that they are not certain that WOLF 424 is indeed IUMMA because of certain discrepancies in characteristics. Our estimates of the surface temperature of WOLF 424 are lower than that of IUMMA, and there is some uncertainty regarding the apparent brightness of IUMMA as seen from earth, due to intervening cosmic dust clouds.

"IUMMA," they go on to explain, "displays alterations in its magnetic field which are very difficult to predict a long time in advance. The detectable intensity of this field as registered by us on UMMO is . . . between a low level of 3.8 Gauss and 215 Gauss." These high levels of magnetism have affected their planet in several ways. The atmosphere is more strongly ionized so that the surface is more insulated from outside radiation than the surface of earth, which means that there have been fewer mutations, therefore fewer varieties of living forms. Another effect has been that they have not been able to use radio as a means of communication on the surface of their planet as easily as we can. "Our early technical history shows that our brother forebears employed great metallic toroids laid out over the countryside (and even today remains of the cables are found where they were buried in those times). In those great metallic toroids intense electrical currents of aperiodic character were induced and the energy stored for future use (in a similar way to the use of your batteries.)"

They describe their planet, UMMO, as follows:

Its morphology can be likened to an ellipsoid of revolution, the radii of which are:

Maximum R	*7251.608 10^3m (kilometers)*
Minimum R	*7016.091 10^3m (kilometers)*

The global mass is: m 9.36 10^{24} Kg.

This describes a planet slightly larger, and more than 50 percent heavier, than earth, whose maximum radius is 6,378 kilometers, compared with 7,251 for UMMO, and whose mass is 5.98×10^{24} Kg, compared with 9.36×10^{24} Kg for UMMO.

"Inclination to the normal in the plane of the ecliptic: 18°39′56.3″ (it undergoes a periodic variation of 19.8 sexagesimal seconds of arc). Note that we are using units familiar to the technicians of earth." (Earth's inclination, the axis tilt that causes seasons, is 23°27′.)

They go on to give the force of gravity on their planet's surface as causing an acceleration of 11.9 meters per second per second, or 20 percent greater than that on the surface of earth, which means that they would feel lighter and stronger here than at home. The UMMO day, or XII, they say, is about 20 percent longer than ours, equal to 30.92 earth hours, which they divide into 600 units called UIW.

The geological structure of UMMO is different from that of earth in that it consists of nine layers (XOODIUMMO DUU OII); and they provide a sketch of a cross-section of UMMO together with descriptions of the chemical compositions of the different layers. One of the most important of the layers, the sixth (the fifth cover to UMMO's core) "has a thickness of approximately 28.8 KOAE (251 kilometers), possessing great diamond-bearing beds, it presents an alveolar (honeycomb) structure in which there remain enormous IOIXOINOYAA (geological concavities) wherein, preserved from the great pressures undergone by the adjacent zones, there are vast quantities of solid, liquid, and gaseous organic substances, especially methane, propane, and oxygen. The chief volcanic activity, as you would term it, occurs in the OAKEDEEI which throw up great fiery columns of these gases toward the surface strata."

The surface of the planet has a single continent, which covers 38 percent of the surface. At the surface level (XOODIUMMO OANMAA) the atmosphere is similar to that of the earth.

The path of UMMO around IUMMA is "an elliptical (almost circular) path with an eccentricity of 0.0078.... The mean distance between UMMO and IUMMA is 9.96×10^{12} cms." This means it is only about two thirds as far from its sun as earth is from its sun. Since UMMO is closer to IUMMA than earth is to its sun and since IUMMA is cooler than our sun, the surface temperature of UMMO is close to that of earth. UMMO's year is shorter than earth's year because UMMO is closer to its sun, just as the year of Venus, closer to our sun, is shorter than earth's.

UMMO apparently does not have a moon. Its year is divided into units called XEE's, which are equal to .212 earth years. It takes three XEE's for UMMO to make one complete orbit around IUMMA. The UMMO year, therefore, is equivalent to three times .212 or .636 of an earth year, or 231 days.

The mass of the star IUMMA is given as 1.48×10^{33} grams (compared with 1.996×10^{33} grams for our sun); and the distance between IUMMA and the sun on July 8, 1967, as 14.421 light years.

An examination of these computations and descriptions reveals that they are all physically consistent with our understanding of celestial mechanics and the characteristics of stars. The lesser mass of IUMMA would give it a lower surface temperature, and the lesser distance of UMMO from IUMMA would enable the planet to have a surface temperature comparable to earth's. The 14.21 light-year distance between the two stars explains why signals broadcast by the Norwegian ships in February, 1934, reached UMMO in 1948, fourteen years later.

What do UMMITES look like? One of the Spanish recipients of UMMO reports received a letter from the man who claimed to be preparing the mimeographed copies of the UMMO statements. He explained that he had been engaged by two tall, fair gentlemen of Scandinavian appearance, one of whom, in a singsong voice, presented the pair as Danish doctors. The duplicating-machine operator had thought nothing in particular about his customers until, in dictating one of their "scientific" reports to him, one of the "doctors" stated that "We come from a cold celestial body called UMMO, which is 14.6 (sic) light years from the earth...."

After finishing the report, the "Danish doctor," sensing the copyist's alarm, told him not to be afraid. He then proceeded to further terrify the copyist by showing him a small sphere that remained stationary in the air and played back, in pictures and sound, a scene that had taken place between the copyist and his wife in his office the preceding day. "This is one of our many methods of observing from a distance," the "doctor" explained.

When talking to the engineer Villagrasa Novoa on the telephone, the strangers answered all his questions with a thoroughness and precision that caused Novoa to think he was conversing either with a computer or with beings reading from an encyclopedia. In addition to providing scientific descriptions of their planet and star, they offered papers on the structure of the physical universe and on philosophical subjects.

In a report on IBOZOO UU (new concepts of space), they stated that earthlings' view of space is "simplistic and not corresponding at all to the true reality of the Cosmos" because it is based on mathematical and geometrical abstractions. Our Euclidian, three-dimensional space, they say, is purely a mental creation; and even with time added as a fourth dimension, as in the theory of relativity, our ideas are superficial. Space, they state, has innumerable dimensions of which they themselves are acquainted with at least ten.

They state that the subatomic particles that we are so busily hunting are an illusion, and that there exist in space folds or warps that make it possible for them to take shortcuts without following "the illusory straight lines on which light travels." They are thus able to cover the more than 14 light years between their star and ours in about eight or nine months.

In a philosophical paper filled with their own terminology, the UMMITES explained that beings like themselves or us (OEMMII) create external "reality" the WAAM, when they think of it. "The external reality if bent in conformance with our mental process, is modified as soon as we focus our consciousness upon it." But this is not to say that beyond this there does not exist a Creator (WOA, God), whose thoughts have "no connection with our thinking processes as dimensional beings."

It is interesting that we have papers and reports of conversations of a scientific or philosophical character, all transmitted through the hands of middle-level engineers, doctors, or lawyers, or "flying saucer" fans, but no attempts at offering genuine evidence of the existence of the UMMITES in the form, say, of advanced hardware or of precise formulas that can be tested by experiment.

The UMMITES' explanation of this is that they are here only as passive observers or students, morally bound not to interfere with our development, by offering "new doctrines . . . new mathematical concepts, or . . . panaceas for social or pathological ills." It suits them, they say, that their statements are not credited. "You can disbelieve us," they write. "You can treat these concepts with mistrust. For the time being do not divulge them among the mass-communication media. You can even show yourselves skeptical in front of those OEMMII (men) who are unfamiliar with your science (which science is analyzing these facts), but do not destroy these printed sheets. Along with a few thousand other sheets, which have been secretly distributed, they constitute the historical beginnings of the first relations between our two hominid systems."

What we have here, apparently, are beings who wish to be hidden yet known, who demonstrate an ability to spy on us, yet claim to be morally bound not to interfere "except in foreseeable and limited cases." It is also demonstrable that nothing in their papers could not have been produced by any competent science-fiction writer. We shall return to this curious business later.

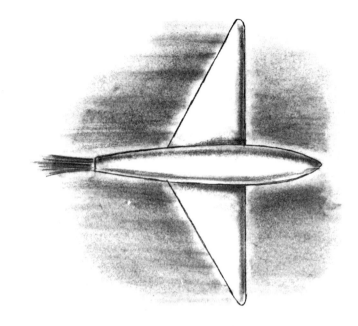

I.

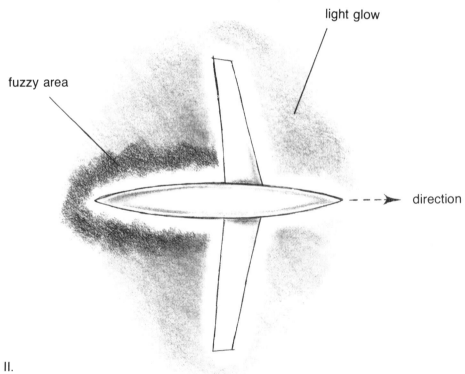

II.

3

The Ships– Eyewitness Reports

♦ ♦ ♦ ♦ ♦ ♦ ♦ ♦ ♦ ♦ ♦ ♦ ♦ ♦ ♦ ♦ ♦ ♦ ♦ ♦

The UMMITES had arrived here, they said, on a lenticular-shaped spaceship, an OAWOLEA UEWA OEM. Lenticular shaped means lens shaped, a "flying saucer." Many of the little people traveled in disks of from 10 to 50 feet in diameter. Signora Lotti's elves had a spindle-shaped craft, José Antonio da Silva's, a spool-shaped one; and Mr. Indrid Cold used a ship shaped like a kerosene lantern. Vehicles of a variety of shapes and sizes have been seen in our skies for many years. Sometimes they fly in a straight line like a conventional aircraft, but they also often exhibit strange maneuvers—wobbling in flight, stopping abruptly, making sharp, right-angle turns, suddenly accelerating, swaying like a pendulum, or hopping up and down like the ball that is followed in sing-along movie strips. Even curiouser, they sometimes emit numbers of smaller shapes, or lights, that dance around them, or even divide themselves into smaller pieces that may later recombine.

Two large objects were seen hovering and flying around a balloon at 112,000 feet altitude in daylight over Artesia, New Mexico. Watched by six observers at two different locations, the two white objects, in one instance, flew towards the 110 foot diameter balloon from the northwest,

I. Seen on the ground by airport-tower operators, and from a commercial airliner. It was shaped something like a large airplane but had no engine pods in the wings. (Sioux City, Iowa, January 20, 1951, 8:26 P.M.)

II. These flew overhead in groups of two to nine. Each glowed red and was surrounded by a luminous red halo. (April 20, 1952, 9:15 to 10:40 P.M.)

circled it, and went off to the northeast. They appeared twice as wide as the balloon and were apparently disk shaped, for they temporarily disappeared while turning as if, in banking, they went edgewise. The witnesses were two members of the General Mills Aeronautical Research Laboratory's balloon project, and four civilian pilots. (January 16, 1952.)

A large white round object was seen between three and four in the morning between Sturgis and Deadwood, South Dakota, on September 22, 1966. For much of the time it hung motionless in the sky. It blacked out when a police car spotlight was directed on it, then came back when the light was turned off. It changed color from pale green, to red, to white, and was approached by two much smaller white objects that came from different directions and stopped nearby. While the two small lights stood still, the large light moved right, down, left, and up, making a square and shooting shafts of blue light towards the ground. Half an hour later, the two small lights flew off at high speed in the directions from which they had come. The large light remained motionless, emitting shafts of blue light, then moved off erratically—stopping, backing up, going forward again, and finally disappearing to the southeast. The witnesses were police officers and operators of police radios at other locations.

III. Shiny and metallic, with protruding round cups, this object was seen in a flat glide path at an altitude of 30 feet, over Indianapolis, Indiana, on July 29, 1948, at 9:55 A.M.

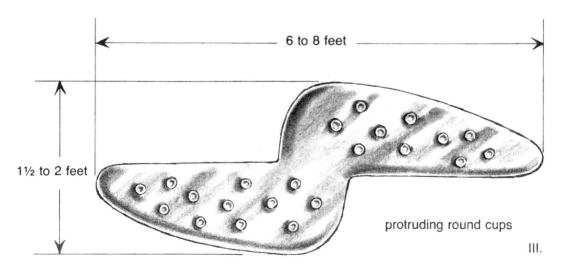

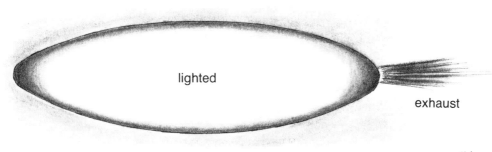

IV.

IV. Appeared transparent and illuminated from the inside and had an exhaust at one end. There were two, one of which hovered while the other moved east and returned. After they rejoined, they ascended until they could no longer be seen. (July 19, 1952, midnight.)

A mother and five children paced 50 feet below a 20 x 8 foot football-shaped object that slowly flew over their Illinois farm one afternoon. The surface was metallic and had longitudinal seams, a small dorsal fin in the rear, and a rectangular black opening near the front. A brownish-gold design was seen on the bottom. The object was surrounded by a thick bluish haze extending about 5 feet in every direction and containing many bubbles or sparks. They heard a strange vibrating noise when they were closest to the object, but felt no signs of electricity. An hour and ten minutes later, when it was dark, another witness, 7 miles away, saw a blue light of the same size and shape moving in the same direction. (Newton, Illinois, October 10, 1966.)

On a clear morning of March 6, 1966, a lady driving in Missouri saw a bright beam of light ahead, a bit broader than the road, shortly after her St. Bernard, who had been sleeping in back, jumped onto the front seat, barking. As they approached the light, the dog whimpered and tried to hide under the dashboard, and the driver noticed that the road beyond the light seemed distorted, as if by heat waves. When they entered the beam, the car slowed from 50 to 10 miles an hour. Looking up through the windshield, the lady saw a bright disk overhead, apparently of metal,

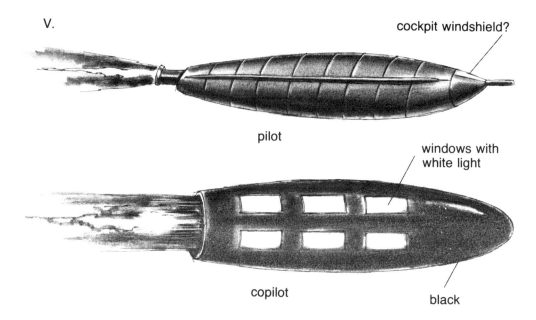

V. This passed a DC-3 in flight over Montgomery, Alabama, and was seen by the pilot, the copilot, and a passenger. (July 24, 1948, 3:40 A.M.)

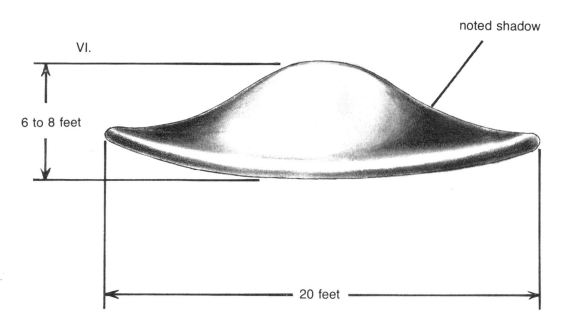

VI. Flew straight and level from horizon to horizon. (July 31, 1948, 8:25 A.M.)

with some sort of dome on top. She could see no real details. Having passed through the beam, the car picked up speed. She did not again look at the disk, which was painfully bright, but her eyes bothered her for three days.

On the night of October 19, 1973, a helicopter piloted by Captain Lawrence J. Coyne encountered a cigar-shaped UFO 1,500 feet over the outskirts of Cleveland, Ohio, at the same time that its radio blacked out. The object had a hull on top, a steady glowing red light on its leading edge and a green light aft, and was headed on a collision course. Captain Coyne descended to avoid it, but the object changed its direction too. Then, at 1,500 feet, the UFO stopped 500 feet above the helicopter and banked to one side. The next thing the Captain and the three others in the crew knew, their altitude was 3,800 feet.

Astronauts in orbit around earth have spotted unknown objects on three occasions. They have never been explained, despite various attempts to do so. The Condon Committee, set up by the Air Force in 1966 to study "flying saucers," tried to explain what Pete Conrad on Gemini 11

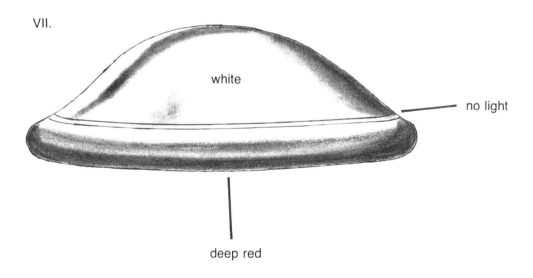

VII. While flying level it appeared to be white, but when it rolled it displayed a red side. Obviously similar to Number VI, shown on page 42.

reported as "a wingman flying wing on us going into sunset here, off to my left. A large object ... tumbling at about one revolution per second. ..." It was, they claimed, the U.S. Proton 3 satellite, which, at the time, was 450 kilometers from Gemini 11's position over Tananarive, Madagascar. The identification of the object as Proton 3 was made by the Condon Committee's photoanalyst. When it was pointed out that the photoanalyst's estimates of the size and distance of the figure established

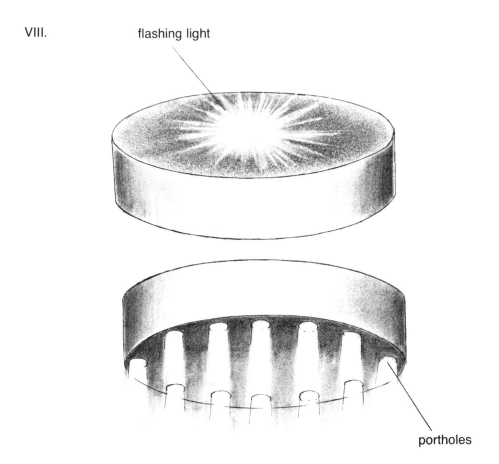

VIII. One hundred feet in diameter, this object was seen by two pilots of a commercial aircraft from a distance of about half a mile. The top center light blinked three times a second and was too bright to look at. The bottom, with its circular portholes, was seen as the object passed in front of the airliner. The interior light, as revealed by the ports, was purplish. It flew in a straight line without spinning, at an estimated speed of more than 1,000 miles an hour. (March 20, 1950, 9:26 P.M.)

that the object could not have been the Proton 3, the photoanalyst retracted his opinion. The object remains a mystery.

Project Blue Book Number 14, one of a series of papers published by the Air Force, which preceded the Condon Committee in investigating "flying saucers," was a report on 4,834 sightings of objects seen in the skies between 1953 and 1955. The Blue Book staff prepared sketches of a dozen of what it considered the best-described sightings.

IX.

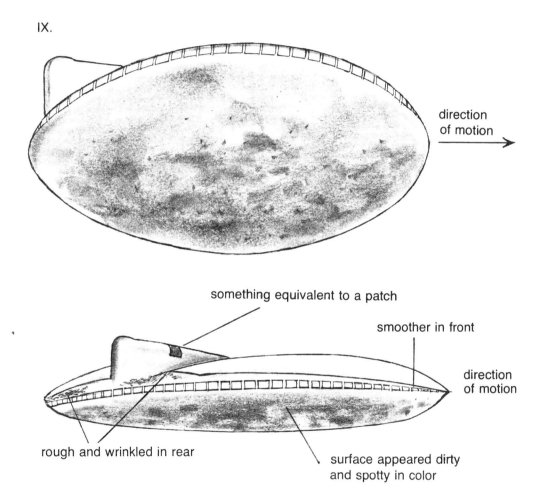

IX. Appeared to reflect sunlight when seen with the naked eye, but did not glare when viewed through binoculars, which revealed a dirty, metallic skin. Horizontal flight at gradually increasing velocity. (May 24, 1949, 5:00 P.M.)

X.

side view

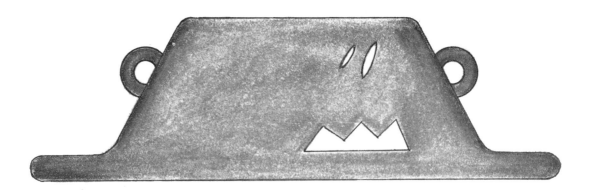

end view

X. Seen hedge-hopping, following the contour of the ground at an altitude of 75 feet, against a canyon wall. It was sky blue, 20 feet in diameter, and 10 feet high. It had pods on the side from which flames shot out. Trees waved when the object flew over them. *(August 13, 1947, 1:00 P.M.)*

XI.

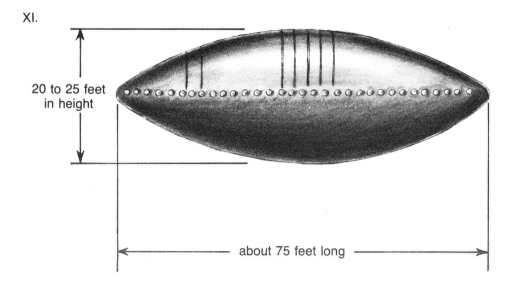

XI. A blue light shone through one of the front windows of this vehicle, which was a dull aluminum color. The head and shoulders of a man were seen through another window. There was much irregular movement in the midsection, which the observer could not understand. It also changed colors. A series of propellers, 6 to 12 inches in diameter, were spaced close together and attached to a bracket along the outer edge, revolving around the object as they spun. It hovered 10 feet over a field, causing vegetation to blow about, then climbed straight up until it could no longer be seen. (August 21, 1952, 5:35 A.M.)

A study of 746 UFO observations by an independent civilian group, NICAP (National Investigation Committee of Aerial Phenomena), found that most could be classified in one of ten basic shapes:

1. *Flat disk (see Central Australian sighting, page 30)*
2. *Domed disk (see VI and VII on pages 42 and 43)*
3. *Double-domed disk (see Boaini sighting on page 8)*
4. *Hemispherical disk, like a half moon*
5. *Flattened shape, sometimes with peaked top (see McMinnville photo, on page 71)*
6. *Spherical (see photo on page 64)*
7. *Egg or football-shaped (see XI above)*
8. *Cylindrical or cigar-shaped (see IV on page 41)*
9. *Triangular or tear-drop shaped*
10. *Single point of light*

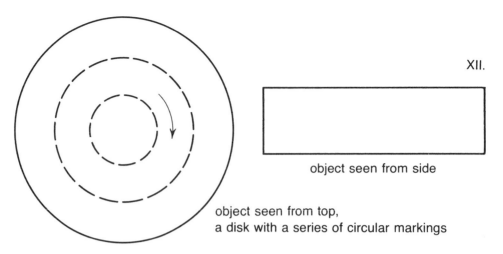

XII. Flew in a series of spinning and tumbling motions over an Air Force Base in Korea—very erratic, flying level, stopping, shooting straight up, flying level, tumbling, changing course. (June 6, 1952, 8:42 A.M.)

Other forms less frequently reported were dumbbell shaped, boomerang shaped (see III on page 40 and photograph on page 49), pear shaped, and possessing three concentric rings (see VII on page 43). Of 746 UFO's, 50 of those seen at night were reported as having windows or portholes, illuminated from within, and outside lights. On a few occasions they were seen to change shape, from "a very bright ... needle, solid and sharply outlined" to a "flattened oval ... not sharply outlined ... and ... duller in color," or to form, or vanish. For example, a "short 'vapor trail' became a brilliant source of light," which diminished to a dull red orange, as its fuzzy appearance "took on a solid look, in the distinct shape of a pencil or a slender cigar." And on another occasion, a pilot saw a brilliantly glowing red object land in a wooded area outside Vera, Texas. When, following the pilot's directions, local police drove to within 100 yards of the object, whose glow had been diminishing, it suddenly disappeared.

UFO's, when observed fairly close up, often create electrical disturbances. Sometimes the radio of a nearby automobile goes dead; at other times the ignition system is affected and the motor stops; sometimes everything electrical fails, including the headlights. Observers have reported a sensation of cold, of heat, or of tingling on the surface of the skin; and afterwards they have often found their faces "sun-burned" and their eyes irritated.

Visually sighted UFO's have, several times, also been detected by radar. In the summer of 1956, several round white objects were tracked over Greenwich, England, by air-traffic-control radars at Lakenheath and Sculthorp RAF stations, while simultaneously seen from the ground and from fighter aircraft that tried to intercept them. First observed at 10:55 P.M., traveling west at 2,000 to 4,000 miles per hour, they then proceeded to start and stop, going from a stationary position to another point, 8 or 20 miles away, at about 600 miles an hour. When a fighter aircraft approached, the light swiftly circled behind it. At other times, the objects made right-angle changes of direction at high speed.

It is strange, however, that almost no unidentified radar echoes have been picked up by the "electronic fence" that stretches across the continental United States. The Space Detection and Tracking System (SPADATS), designed to keep track of all objects in orbit in the near space around earth and on ballistic (free-fall) trajectories, and sensitive enough to detect objects the size of nails, would automatically register any space ship, whether earth-based or alien.

A newspaper reporter photographed this boomerang-shaped light through a telescope as it flew over Clovis, New Mexico, on January 23, 1976.

4

The Anatomy of the Strangers

◆ ◆ ◆ ◆ ◆ ◆ ◆ ◆ ◆ ◆ ◆ ◆ ◆ ◆ ◆ ◆ ◆

As we have seen, strange visitors are often associated with odd-looking flying machines. On the other hand, when strange objects are observed only in flight, it is usually impossible to tell whether they are "manned" (an occupant is mentioned in only one of the twelve Blue Book cases, number XI). There are also a number of observations of visitors without "ships" (the UMMITES and the goblins of Hopkinsville, Kentucky—although there had been reports of "flying saucers" in the vicinity of Hopkinsville). In other words, visitors are not always associated with vehicles. For all we know, many of the "flying saucers" seen in the sky are uninhabited, and many of the visitors may have reached here by other means.

Let us take a closer look at these strange visitors. In her book *Flying Saucer Occupants*, Mrs. Coral Lorenzen of APRO (Aerial Phenomena Research Organization) lists ninety-eight reports of pilots or crews of peculiar vehicles. With the exception of one report from 1914, all are for the years 1947 to 1966. The reports are classified according to the time of day of the sightings, the type of "ship," and the appearance of the occupant.

Of the ninety-eight reports, forty-six, or almost half, were of small "humanoids" under 40 inches tall; and thirty-two, or a third, were of normal-sized "humanoids." Of the remaining twenty, four were small robots, two were large robots, six were monsters of various sizes, and eight were either not described or, as farmer Hamilton found (page 75). indescribable. Of the half of the forty-six dwarfs whose garb was described, nine wore "diving suits"; nine wore unusual clothes—tight leggings, jackets and cloaks, for example—and five wore ordinary clothing. One, though, had a "diving helmet."

In only ten cases (less than a quarter), did the observers report on the appearance of the dwarfs. Of these, nine said that their eyes were large, and one said they were glowing. In only four cases were there descriptions of hands—one stated that they appeared normal, and three that they had claws. Both normal hands and claws were associated with large eyes, although the one glowing-eyed dwarf had claws.

As we must assume that most of the dwarfs who were not clearly seen resembled those that were, we would have to say that probably all the dwarfs had large or glowing eyes and that many had claws.

As might be expected, a higher proportion of the larger visitors was clearly described. Whereas the clothing of only half the dwarfs was reported, that of three quarters of the larger visitors was. Of the twenty-four large "humanoids," half were reported as wearing "diving suits" (which, of course, could be space-suits), four, as wearing something unusual, and seven as in ordinary clothing—suits, coveralls, and so on. Reports on the eyes of the large "humanoids" were more frequent too. Almost half of the larger types' eyes (fourteen) were seen, as opposed to less than a quarter of those of the dwarfs. Of these fourteen, half had normal eyes, six had large eyes, and one had glowing eyes. Three were observed to have normal hands and one to have claws (he also had over-sized eyes), indicating perhaps that the larger "humanoids," unlike the dwarfs, were more likely to have hands than claws. Both types of "humanoid" are three times as likely to be seen at night, or in the dimness of twilight or dawn, than to be seen in daylight.

MUFON (Midwest UFO Network), another volunteer group, has classified visitors more thoroughly, employing its own interviews with persons who have seen them and careful studies of other reports. With this information, MUFON member Hayden C. Hewes of Oklahoma City has broken the visitors down into four broad groups: dwarfs, "human" types in our size range, hairy creatures, and others (glowing, shapeless, partly or wholly invisible).

Type 1, the dwarf group, can, Hewes says, vary in skin color from "translucent" to white, gray, bluish, or glossy black. MUFON has, he says, found no reports of such beings possessing pinkish or brownish "human colors"; nor has it found anyone who says they have green skins. Descriptions of them as "little green men," MUFON believes, probably comes from the color of their suits or of the flowing lights they move around in.

Basically, Type 1 is from 3 to 4 feet tall with an abnormally large head and high forehead, with large and wide-set eyes that can rivet one's attention with an intense stare. Eye color varies from jet black to dark blue, yellow, or glowing. The ears can vary from inconspicuous to very large; the nose from near human to slits. The jaw is small and the chin pointed.

Type 1 alien, a drawing based on numerous descriptions from many different parts of the world. This specimen is depicted in what some observers say is a "diving suit"—probably a space suit. Others wear cloaks and trousers or coveralls, and even caps with feathers.

Type 1's arms are long and thin. Their hands may be like those of human beings, but they may have varying numbers of fingers or claws or tendrils. The shoulders are broad and the footprints often peculiar, like those of an elephant or other hoofed animal.

Some Type 1's have misshapen bodies, with one arm higher than the other, or uneven eyes. They have been seen collecting geological and biological specimens, including humans, and repairing and maintaining their "ships." When waved at, they usually wave back, but tend to shyly withdraw when approached. When interfered with, they can paralyze humans with a light-beam weapon. MUFON adds that the Type 1's never offer information to people, and are seen only at night or in dim light, which would indicate that their large eyes are adapted to darkness.

Interestingly, MUFON finds no sharp dividing line between Type 1's and Type 2's. They seem to melt into each other, as if by elongating a Type 1 it appears more and more human until, at around 6 feet in height, it is almost indistinguishable from *homo sapiens*. The one characteristic of Type 2's reported by all who have encountered them is that their complexions are dark or heavily tanned. There is also always, no matter how "normal" they appear, something odd about them, something indescribable that gives the sense of an alien presence. Contrary to Mrs. Lorenzen's reports, MUFON states that the Type 2's wear coveralls or fatigues more often than "diving suits."

Unlike the Type 1's, the Type 2's are communicative, often annoyingly so. They offer stories of their homelands, and give reasons for their visits. Often they foretell the future. One is reported to have predicted Robert Kennedy's death. They come bearing tidings of misfortunes that shall overwhelm earth if men do not change their ways. They describe their home worlds as paradises free of the scourges that plague mankind. On other occasions, they had been reported to be harassing investigators of UFO's or those who have just reported their landings. They come unannounced, bearing strange, incomprehensible forms to be filled out; telephone at odd hours; tell people to keep quiet about what they have seen; misrepresent themselves as government agents, and so on. They are suspected of living amongst us in ordinary clothes, which, however, are

Type 2 alien resembles an Earthman, but an uncanny sensation is felt by those who meet him, and his breathing is frequently labored. Sometimes he wears an ordinary black business suit with a necktie, and carries a briefcase. Some Type 2 aliens have tentacles instead of hands.

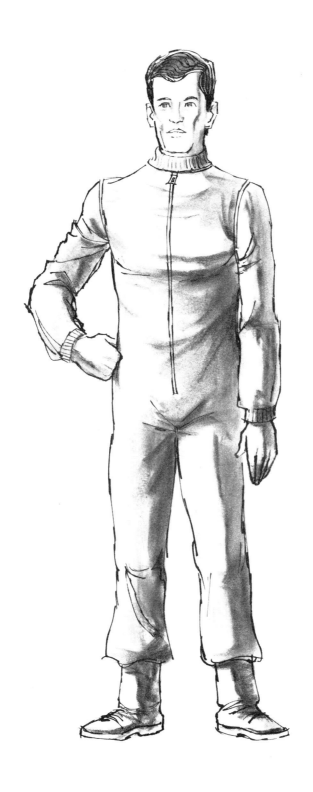

Type 3 aliens are spooky-looking and act more like apes than people. They come in different sizes and sometimes have just one eye in the center of their foreheads.

always black. They have a vaguely oriental look, and high cheekbones. Their fingers are long, and they often speak in a mechanical fashion, wheezing between words because of some breathing difficulty.

Type 3's are hairy bipeds varying in height from 2 feet to over 7 feet. They have huge shapeless heads, glowing orange eyes, long arms with claws, and sometimes run on all fours. Their behavior is on a par with that of chimpanzees. The sometimes invisible, or evanescent, or shape-changing Type 4's, MUFON finds unclassifiable due to a scarcity of information.

What else do we know about these visitors?

The five tables on the following pages all refer to the same cases —nineteen sightings of UFO's and occupants in Spain and Portugal. Table 4 shows that the same types of aliens in about the same proportions are found in these cases as in Mrs. Lorenzen's ninety-eight world-wide cases. (Another study of fifty-one Latin American reports gives a similar breakdown: thirty dwarfs, fourteen of normal size, and seven giants.)

Sighting					L	W
1.		April 5, 1935	7:30 p.m.	Aznalcazar (Sevilla, Spain). Date approximate	Ω	1
2.	Monday	July 25, 1938	11:30 p.m.	Guadalajara (Spain). Location approximate	@	2
3.		1948		Garganta la Olla (Caceres, Spain)	Ω	1
4.		July 1, 1953	2:00 p.m.	Villares del Saz (Cuenca, Spain). Date approximate	@	1
5.	Friday	June 10, 1960	3:30 a.m.	Algoz (Algarve, Portugal)	@	1
6.		May 16, 1966		Cordoba (Cordoba, Spain). Date approximate	@	1
7.		July 1967	3:00 a.m.	Palma (Palma, Balearic Islands, Spain)	@	1
8.		September 1967	12:30 a.m.	Santa Coloma-La Roca (Barcelona, Spain)	@	1
9.		April 1968		Tossa de Mar (Gerona, Spain) Date approximate	@	s
10.	Friday	August 16, 1968	6:00 a.m.	Serra de Almos (Tarragona, Spain)	Ω	1
11.		August 31, 1968	8:00 p.m.	Santiponce (Sevilla, Spain). Date approximate	@	4
12.	Wednesday	September 11, 1968	11:45 p.m.	San Marti de Tous (Barcelona, Spain)	@	1
13.	Saturday	September 21, 1968	2:00 a.m.	La Llagosta (Barcelona, Spain)	@	1
14.	Saturday	September 21, 1968	3:00 a.m.	La Escala (Gerona, Spain)	@	1
15.	Tuesday	September 24, 1968	9:00 p.m.	Cedeira (La Coruña, Spain)	@	1
16.	Friday	October 11, 1968		Setcases (Gerona, Spain)	@	s
17.	Monday	January 6, 1969	8:30 p.m.	Pontejos (Santander, Spain)	Ω	4
18.	Thursday	January 16, 1969	8:30 p.m.	Las Pajanosas (Sevilla, Spain)	@	1
19.	Friday	February 28, 1969	2:45 a.m.	Miajadas (Caceres, Spain)	@	2

Note and key
These cases are chosen from a catalog of 130 landing reports, updated by V-J. Ballester Olmos in August 1972.
Column L indicates where the object was reported to have touched down (@), or to have come close to the ground (Ω). Column W notes the number of witnesses; s means "several."

Table 1: List of nineteen UFO-occupant cases reported on Iberian Peninsula (Spain and Portugal).

Table 2: Characteristics of UFO's accompanying Iberian visitors.

Sighting	Shape	Size	Color
1.	round	large	most brightly
2.	lens-shaped	11 x 5 meters (about 37 x 16 feet)	dazzling white
3.	ball		fire
4.	egg-shaped	1.30 x 0.62 meters (about 4 x 2 feet)	bright, white or gray
5.			intense luminosity
6.	disk		
7.			intense brightness
8.	sauce-pan	enormous	blinding fluorescence
9.	circular		bright
10.	hemisphere		terrible brightness
11.	round	5 x 5 meters (?) (about 16 x 16 feet)	metallic, one white light on top and two green ones at the ends
12.	ovoidal	5 x 3 meters (about 16 x 10 feet)	red-orange, very brilliant
13.	egg-shaped		very luminous
14.	round, like a buoy		
15.			brightness
16.			
17.	dome, disk base	12 x 6 meters (?) (about 40 x 20 feet)	strong orange
18.	rectangular	large	
19.			

Sighting	Number of Occupants	Voice	Equipment
1.	several		
2.	two		
3.	one	sound of voice	
4.	three	language not understood	dark blue suit and a flat hat with a visor (peak?) in front and a metal sheet on the arm
5.	six		
6.	several		
7.	two		
8.	several		white, brilliant clothes
9.	one		a bright ball was carried in the hand
10.	two		
11.	one		black and brown check shirt and black long trousers
12.	four	soft hissing sound due to movement	
13.	one		
14.	two		black tight-fitting clothes
15.	two		
16.	several		
17.	five		dark suit, tight-fitting at the neck and sleeves
18.	several		
19.	five		

Table 3: Numbers of occupants seen together in Iberia, their voices, and equipment.

Table 4: Descriptions of occupants in the Iberian cases. Of sixteen whose sizes are reported, ten, or about two-thirds, are small. A number have large eyes, and as they approach human size (Number 17) their appearance tends to get less bizarre. Two creatures are monsters.

Sighting	Size	Head	General Appearance
1.	small		
2.			
3.	small		legs ended in "goat's feet"
4.	0.65 meters (about 2 feet 3 inches)	yellowish-greenish face and narrow eyes	cold and brilliant hand
5.			
6.	small		like "green birds." Seemed to be "tired"
7.	"like children"	enormous eyes and large head or helmet	
8.	very small or on knees	large	
9.	tall		
10.	1.50 meters (about 5 feet)		seemed like giant octopuses, 4 or 5 feet across; clear color; repugnant
11.	tall	large eyes	thin
12.	about 1.00 meter (about 3 feet 5 inches)		the "forms" consisted of two balls, one above the other, the bottom one being a little larger. They shone like moonlight with a metallic reflection (like silver). They bounced and hissed. No human appearance
13.	small		
14.		ugly yellowish faces	
15.	very tall	fair "men" wearing, with lights on their foreheads	
16.	"lower than normal"		human appearance
17.	1.80-2.00 meters (about 6 feet to 6 feet 10 inches)	pale face, long dark brown hair	normal appearance, genteel. Arms almost joined to body
18.			"silhouettes" like persons
19.	very tall	"hairless"	"luminous body of humanoid configuration"

Table 5: Behavior of occupants in Iberia.

Sighting
1. The beings moved around the object.
2. They descended in a platform from the object's base. They seemed to be moving. When one of the "forms" raised an arm (?) a circle of bluish light illumined the area. Then the object took off and was lost to sight.
3. It came into a hut in the middle of a storm, approaching the fire. The witness escaped in terror, but he could observe a "ball of fire" elevated not far from there.
4. Three little men got out through a flap in the upper part of the UFO, came close to the witness, and spoke to him. Then, one of them gave the child a little slap in the face and went into the object again, which rose at great speed.
5. The beings were moving around the object. Later, it was seen flying over the area and it disappeared.
6. The occupants went down from the object, but when they realized they were being observed they reentered and the object took off.
7. They were standing at the window of the witness's room and were speaking to each other.
8. The beings tried to climb up the thicket on the right of the road and go towards the object, which landed on the thicket on the left.
9. A UFO descended and landed. A man came out, moved several times around the object, and then reentered it, whereupon it flew away and disappeared.
10. Two strange beings ran towards the object, which they entered by its base a few feet from the ground.
11. A tall man came near the object from an adjoining plantation of olive trees.
12. The "things" quickly climbed the hill towards the object, with springing gait, and disappeared under it. They did not seem to know of the presence of an observer. The object immediately ascended at great speed.
13. The being was beside the landed object.
14. Two beings emerged from the interior of the UFO on to the sea.
15. Two beings came walking along the road, not far from where there was a weird brightness ("like a blaze"). They crossed over to the witness, who was walking in the opposite direction.
16. They emerged from the object when it landed.

17. A being going from right to left several times was seen in a "luminous square." To the right another one appeared and both met on the left. Then three more appeared from the right, and the five beings met in the center. They did not move their arms or incline their bodies.
    Suddenly they vanished along with the luminosity. A dome-shaped object brightened and departed at great speed.
18. The human silhouettes walked several times within the illuminated rectangle.
19. The witnesses saw five beings beside a landed object.

5

Horses, Hattocks, and Kugelblitzes

◆ ◆ ◆ ◆ ◆ ◆ ◆ ◆ ◆ ◆ ◆ ◆ ◆ ◆ ◆ ◆ ◆

Almost three hundred years ago, in the year 1691, a Scotch minister, Robert Kirk, published the results of his research in what he called *The Secret Commonwealth of Elves, Fauns and Fairies*. Many people at that time had experiences with these mysterious beings and were concerned either to avoid or cultivate them or to give them gifts to keep them at bay. Kirk reported that some had bodies like condensed clouds, which could either appear solid or vanish, that they generally were seen best at dusk, and often lived underground in houses equipped with lamps that never went out and fires that burned without fuel. When talking amongst themselves they used whistling sounds, but they could also address humans in their own language and usually dressed in the fashion of the time and place, wearing "plaids and variegated garments in the highlands of Scotland, and suanochs . . . in Ireland." They traveled extensively, Kirk said, could go from one continent to another at great speed, "pierce Cows or other Animals . . . whose substance . . . [they] take to live on," and were invulnerable to human weapons, while their weapons could inflict harm without making a visible wound.

Belief in fairies, elves, gnomes, brownies, and hobgoblins—known by these and many other names—is widespread throughout the world. The fairies of modern children's stories, delicate winged creatures, are a

Object photographed by a policeman as it flew over Sherman, Texas, 17 miles south of the Texas-Oklahoma border. It was between two and three in the morning on a clear night, and appears to be a **kugelblitz (ball lightning).**

recent literary invention. The fairies, or feys, of legend, did not possess wings, although they could fly through the air, and they could be any size, from human to diminutive, with bodies of a cloudlike nature. One might come upon a fey anywhere and think it was human. Its dress would be ordinary and its story plausible. The encounter might seem hardly worth mentioning, except that at the end the fey might just disappear. Sometimes they would capture humans or lure them into their quarters, illuminated by a mysterious, sourceless glow. One curious feature of fairyland was that time did not exist as we know it. A person might spend what he thought was a day in a fairy castle only to learn, when he returned, that all his friends were dead and that centuries had passed. Five minutes of dancing with the fairies might equal a week of mortal time.

Dwarfs, known by different names to American Indians, ancient Greeks, eskimos, and every culture in Europe, Asia, and Africa, were full grown at three and appeared as old gray beards at seven. They had wrinkled, leathery dark skin, wide mouths, green eyes, thick heads, powerful stocky bodies, large hands, arms so long that they almost touched the ground, and walked flat-footed with an uncertain, wobbly gait as a result of the peculiar structure of their feet. They were nocturnal, and were clever with their hands.

Elves were more pleasant to look at. The same size as dwarfs, they were well-proportioned, had a green complexion and luxuriant hair worn over their shoulders. They dressed in green with red caps and white feathers. Hobgoblins, bugs, bogles, or bogys, were less pleasant members of the *Secret Commonwealth*. They often had large glowing eyes as big as saucers, or could be headless or covered with long hair, or assume all sorts of other frightening shapes. The Will o' the Wisp, seen most commonly on autumn evenings after sunset, resembled a flame until, close up, it was seen to be bluish, reddish, greenish, or yellowish, merging into purple. Sometimes it was motionless; at other times it bounded over the countryside, rising high in the air and then descending. On occasion it would divide into several smaller flames that would move in a complicated fashion, sometimes to recombine again.

◆ ◆ ◆ ◆ ◆ ◆

For most of the past century, such things as fairies, elves, brownies, and goblins have been dismissed as "superstition," as folk tales invented by ignorant people to explain perfectly natural phenomena. It was said that Yorkshire peasants, knowing nothing of bacteria, invented an agency to account for the curdling of milk—brownies, who curdled the milk out of spite. The Will o' the Wisp was dismissed as marsh gas, the spontaneous combustion of methane produced by rotting dead animals and plants at the bottom of swamps.

Yet, people have been seeing fairies, dwarfs, elves, goblins, and their ilk—or creatures uncannily like them—in many parts of the world for the past thirty years. The little men who badgered Signora Rosa Lotti could surely be called elves, except for their strange spindle-shaped vehicle. The bearded creatures who kidnapped José Antonio da Silva certainly sound like dwarfs. In fact, every one of the creatures reported to have been seen entering or piloting a "flying saucer" or other unidentified flying object fits the description of one or another of the citizens of the *Secret Commonwealth*. The swarthy Mr. Cold, who met Mr. Derenberger on Route 77, would have been accounted a fey or demon in other times. True, da Silva's dwarfs, unlike those of legend, went about in daylight, but they wore protective suits in the sun, and if we omit the story of the voyage in the little spool, their home fits the description of the legendary dwellings of the dwarfs. It had no windows, so surely could have been underground or in a cave, and there was the same sourceless lighting of the ancient tales as well as a difference in time.

So we have a puzzle. We have demons, knells, trolls, and goblins appearing in the twentieth century, accompanied by flying machines shaped like spindles, spools, saucers, and lanterns. What are we to make of this? Did the goblins seen in the sixteenth century and before hide their flying machines? Or are these modern fairies and elves different from those of ancient times? Were those of old mere fantastic inventions; and are those seen today visitors who, by some strange coincidence, look and behave like our legends?

Let us follow the most likely assumption, that is that the elves of old times and today are the same. Where, then, are they from? Are they, as they now claim, from Mars, Venus, Lanulos in the galaxy of Ganymede, Wolf 424, or somewhere else in space, or are they, as they formerly claimed, from underground, or visitors with "no terrestrial habitations"?

Before trying to answer these questions, let us examine what has become of the fairies of old. A number of researchers, particularly in the British Isles, where such legends abound, have tried to find out. It seems that with the growth in population and spread of industrialism, the secret folk have quitted many of their old haunts. However, in out-of-the-way parts of Scotland and Wales, and on the Isle of Man, Katherine Briggs was able to find a few people who had seen elves and such, 2 or 3 feet high, with red caps and green jackets. One man reported that on a summer day in 1932, near the Glen Alden slate quarries, he had spotted five 18 inch men, gray, the color of fungus, and with protruding bellies, dancing in a ring. William Butterfield of Ikley Wells claimed to have seen a whole crowd of little twittering green men bathing with their clothes on. A clergyman's widow saw a small man in green in Regents Park, London. In 1962, a farmer's wife in Timberscombe, Berkshire Downs, saw a little man in green standing at her elbow; and that same year a professional woman vacationing with her daughter in Cornwall saw a small green man with a pointed hood and ears, standing by a gate. There was something menacing in his aspect. The little girl screamed and she and her mother ran away. (It was generally considered dangerous to be seen by an elf before one saw him.)

◆ ◆ ◆ ◆ ◆ ◆

Whether or not we can believe that present-day gnomes are the same as those that the Reverend Kirk talks about depends on the "flying saucers." If the spindles, spools, disks, and so on that people have been seeing are real machines, then we must assume that our gnomes are not the same, because Kirk's did not have any. No one in Kirk's day described gnomes as landing in whirling machines with flashing lights or claimed that anyone was carried off in such a device. The Reverend did mention that some had "astral bodies, agitated as wildfire with whirlwind"; but such a construction is less substantial than the hard, metallic objects that have been seen on the ground at rest, which whirl only on taking off, if at all.

Kirk's elves rode miniature cream-colored horses with small bells attached to their manes, if they used any form of transportation; and demons in a hurry were known to drive coaches harnessed to strange fiery-eyed steeds whose feet barely touched the ground. In the words of the English antiquarian, John Aubrey, they used "words, Horse and Hattock [a little hat]. . . ." But the favorite means of getting around used by most members of the fairy kingdom was flying, pure and simple, just floating themselves into the air and darting hence with lightninglike speed. "Their chameleon-lyke Bodies," Kirk noted, "swim in the Air near Earth with Bag and Baggage."

So if the saucers and other unidentified flying objects seen with the goblins are real, we must say that our goblins are something new. We cannot believe that the legendary goblins, who could get around adequately without mechanical assistance, would have in the past thirty years or so had to invent machines to transport themselves.

A young man named Ted Phillips, Jr., of MUFON, spends all his spare time investigating physical evidence of landings of UFO's. This evidence consists of circles on the ground, either of flattened vegetation, often in a whirled or radiating (like spokes in a wheel) pattern, or of

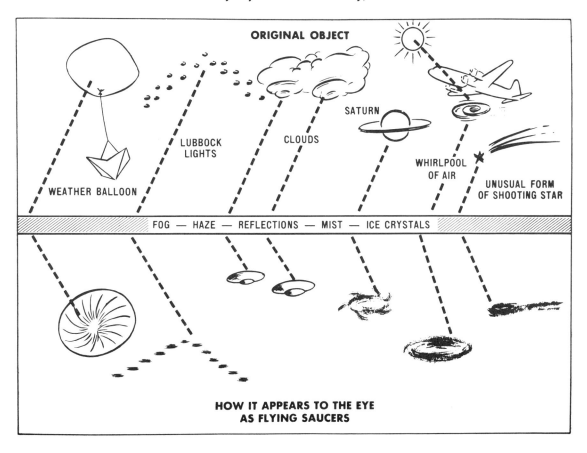

Professor Donald Menzel of Harvard believes all UFO's are illusions. Many, he thinks, are reflections of objects or lights on or near the ground from layers of ice crystals or inversion layers in the sky, which act as mirrors. Others could be eddies of air caused by aircraft. The drawing illustrates some of his theories. The "Lubbock Lights" referred to were photographed flying in formation over Texas at 18,000 miles per hour on August 31, 1951. Optical illusions can account for many objects seen in the sky, but not for all.

scorching or denuding (plants plucked out of the ground by suction); and to a lesser extent of indentations caused by landing gear, or tree branches broken or scorched as the craft enters or leaves the landing area. Of some three hundred landing circles he has cataloged, almost one hundred were associated with objects seen landing by two or more witnesses. Most of the rings are between twenty and thirty feet in diameter, which corresponds with the reported size of most "flying saucers." (There is a consistency in these reports from all over the world that certainly argues that people in different places are seeing the same things.)

In a typical case that occurred in Iowa late one night in July, 1969, two teen-aged girls saw, from their bedroom window, a dark metallic ship spinning counter-clockwise. It was shaped like an inverted bowl with a curved bottom and with a band of reddish-orange light two thirds of the way from the bottom to the top. Shortly after the sighting there was a light rain, and early the next morning, when the girls' father, a farmer, went out to check a field of soybeans, he found a 40 foot circle with all the leaves wilted. As he had been working in the field the previous day, he knew the circle had not been there then. Several weeks later, the field was visited by UFO investigator Allen Hynek, an astronomer of Northwestern University. He found, he wrote, "the leaves of each plant . . . hanging wilted from the stalks as though they had been subjected to intense heat, but the stalks themselves were not broken or bent, and there were no marks of any kind in the soil. Everything appeared as though the heat or destroying agent was applied directly from above and at close range but without direct contact.

This sort of thing is the closest we have to physical evidence that the strange machines, or whatever they are, associated with gnomes and other eerie phantoms really exist. We have no photographs of the spindles, spools, boomerangs, or footballs, and very few of the disk photographs have passed inspection.

With regard to the evidence comprising rings, scorching, and similar phenomena, an aviation writer and former electrical engineer, Philip J. Klass, believes they are related to ball lightning, or *kugelblitz*, a weird and little-understood phenomenon.

The nineteenth-century astronomer Camille Flammarion, the first to scientifically investigate the *kugelblitz*, wrote "In shape they are not always spherical, 'though this is their normal appearance; and although their contours are clearly defined, they are sometimes encircled by a kind of luminous vapor such as is often seen encircling the moon.

Paul Trent took two pictures of this domed disk as it flew over his McMinnville, Oregon, farm on the afternoon of May 11, 1950. After examining the photographs with great care, the Air Force's Condon Committee could find no reason to doubt their authenticity (unlike many other "flying saucer" photos, which were proven to be fakes). This picture is one of the few instances of evidence of the existence of the strange flying machines.

"Sometimes they are furnished with a red flame like a fuse that has been lit. Sometimes they leave behind them a luminous trail which remains visible after they themselves have disappeared. They have been described as looking like a crouching kitten, an iron bar, a large orange.... There is a record of one being seen as large as a mill stone (about 20 feet in diameter). One remarkable thing about them is the slowness with which they move, and which sometimes enables their course to be watched for several minutes." They often flew with a rocking motion like a falling leaf, and appeared to grow larger as they ascended.

Flammarion listed a number of *kugelblitz* sightings. A painter named Batti saw one in Milan in June, 1841, which appeared to be "the size and color of the moon rising above the Alps on a clear winter night." He reported it as reddish yellow with patches of red and surrounded by a glowing atmosphere, indefinite in extent. On November 12, 1887, "an enormous fireball was seen to rise slowly out of the sea to the height of fifty feet. It traveled against the wind and came quite close to the vessel from which it was being watched. Then it turned towards the southeast and disappeared." (Off Cape Race, Newfoundland.)

In going over reports on *kugelblitz* observations, Klass found that their colors corresponded with those of "flying saucers." The most common colors, both of ball lightning and "saucers," are red, orange, and red-orange. Next in frequency are blue, white, and blue-white. In one of the best-documented reports on "saucer" sightings, writer John Fuller reported that at Exeter, New Hampshire, some exhibited red, green, and white lights in combination. A survey of ball lightning revealed that 27 percent also displayed combinations of two or three colors. The floating, bouncing, or random motion reported by a quarter of the *kugelblitz* observers also corresponded to the motions ascribed to "saucers"; and both often appeared to be spinning or rolling.

Although forms of ball lightning have been produced in the laboratory, no one knows how they are formed in nature or exactly what they are. It is known that they are often seen after thunderstorms, and associated with tornadoes, which may, in fact, be basically electrical storms. Klass believes that they can be produced by high-powered radio and radar transmissions and by high-tension power lines. Many "saucer" sightings are near power lines (which often run along roads) and some large glowing circular objects have actually been photographed on power grids. Klass also suspects, based on some theories that certain gases may help form *kugelblitzes*, that exhausts from automobiles or fertilizers on farms might contribute to their formation, which would account for sightings like those of the two girls in Iowa. The devastated circle on the soybean field, for example, could have been caused by the great heat *kugelblitzes* are reported to generate. And the electrical nature of the *kugelblitz* would account for many of the things reported to happen when people see "saucers": tingling, hair standing on end, radios going dead, car engines stalling. *Kugelblitzes* can generate very powerful light that is not confined to the visible spectrum, which could account both for the great brightness reported by "saucer" observers, and their sensitive, watering eyes, which could be suffering the effects of exposure to ultraviolet, and their difficulty in describing the exact appearance of the object. (See the sighting by the lady driving in Missouri with her St. Bernard dog, page 41.) Many observers, Klass believes, state that the UFO's have a metallic skin because they are accustomed to seeing reflected sunlight flashing from what they know to be the aluminum skins of aircraft. They interpret the bright, self-generated glow of the *kugelblitz* as sunlight reflected from a metal surface. As what they are seeing is not what they think it is, they become confused when they get a closer look, stating that the UFO's surface resembles "sand-blasted . . . weathered" or dirty aluminum. One observer reported that a UFO was "silvery on top, but bright orange underneath, possibly reflecting sunlight" although the sun could not have been reflected from the underside.

If, as seems likely, it is necessary for a *kugelblitz* to rotate, this would account for the spinning motion of many UFO's, and also for their shapes, which almost always have the symmetry of objects formed by rotation, as on a potter's wheel. It would also account for their erratic movements, which resemble those of a gyroscope.

A good example of how a *kugelblitz* can mystify observers, and even lead to reports of occupants, can be seen in an episode that occurred on June 22, 1976, on Grand Canary Island. At 10:30 P.M., Dr. Francisco Padron and his driver saw a sphere the size of a three story building (30 feet in diameter) about 60 yards off the road. "It was," the doctor reported, "of a grayish blue color, but transparent—we could see stars right through it.

"It was suspended a few feet off the ground.

"There were two figures toward the center of the sphere. They were well over six feet tall.

"They were either dressed in brilliant red or red in color.

"Their faces were flesh-colored and human in appearance. I could not see any ears because they wore a kind of helmet or clothlike helmet on their heads.

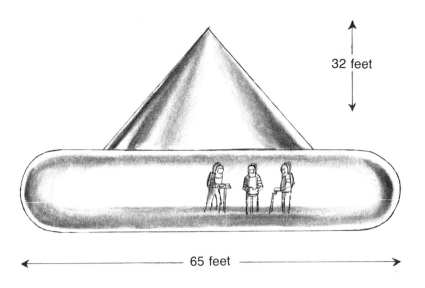

*This craft with three figures inside is probably a **kugelblitz**, as perceived by a Spanish farmer.*

"Their heads gave off a glow, like a halo or an aura.

"They had pointed, winglike appendages on the end of their arms that moved slowly, like hands. They seemed intent on some sort of control panel.

"Suddenly the car radio went dead and we felt a terrible coldness. The object began to lift off—and seemed to be growing steadily larger as it rose!"

We can see that this sighting exhibits many of the characteristics of a *kugelblitz*: the outlines are indefinite and in fact stars can be seen through at least the outer portions (the luminous atmosphere); it moves slowly and appears to swell as it rises; it produces radio interference. But what about the "human-shaped" figures seen by Dr. Padron?

We would be left only with the doctor's word for them had there not been other observers. Fortunately, the object was seen by a number of other persons, including Domingo Alamo, an architectural draftsman, and Dr. Fernando Bello, an astronomer at a nearby observatory. Neither Alamo nor Bello saw any "human-shaped" figures. Alamo saw "a perfectly round, transparent sphere in the center of which was a *sort of bent, long shape of a bright color.*" Dr. Bello, along with other members of the observatory staff, saw a "giant, brilliant sphere *with a swirling center shaped like a snail.*" (Author's italics.)

If, as seems probable, we can dismiss the circles, scorched or otherwise, the broken tree limbs, and soil indentations as the work of ball lightning, then there remains as evidence for various strange machines only the descriptions of eyewitnesses.

Eyewitnesses of elves and fairies of centuries past, we have seen, reported sighting not machines with these beings, but horses and coaches. If a Brazilian soldier in 1969 sees a spool-shaped machine with his gnomes, and an Irish farmer in 1724 sees a small coach and four with his, we might suspect that what one sees a gnome riding in has something to do with one's own knowledge and expectations. What would have happened, for example, had feys been spotted say eighty or ninety years ago, before the era of DC 3's, Boeing 707's, or space travel?

Interestingly enough, we have a number of sightings from the late years of the nineteenth century. What did these people see?

On the night of April 21, 1897, a well-known and prosperous Kansas farmer, bearing the famous name Alexander Hamilton, was awakened by a noise made by his cattle. With his son and a hired man he went out to investigate. They saw an airship slowly descend, to hover 50 feet overhead.

"It consisted of a great cigar-shaped portion," Hamilton later swore in an affidavit, "possibly 300 feet long, with a carriage underneath. The carriage was made of glass or some other transparent substance alternating with a narrow strip of some material. It was brilliantly lighted within and everything was plainly visible—it was occupied by six of the strangest beings I ever saw. They were jabbering together, but we could not understand a word they said."

When they spotted Hamilton and his companions, the crew did something and the ship rose to 300 feet.

"It seemed to pause and hover over a two-year-old heifer, which was bawling and jumping, apparently fast in the fence. Going to her, we found a cable about a half-inch in thickness made of some red material, fastened in a slip knot around her neck, one end passing up to the vessel, and the heifer tangled in the wire fence. We tried to get it off, but could not, so we cut the wire loose and stood in amazement to see the ship, heifer and all, rise slowly, disappearing in the northwest.

Hamilton spent a frightened, sleepless night and, the next day made an unsuccessful search for the heifer. That night a neighbor, Link Thomas, who lived 3 or 4 miles to the west, found the animal's hide, legs, and head in his field, noting a strange absence of foot or hoofprints in the vicinity of the remains. Hamilton kept having nightmares of the ship with its big light and "cursed people. I don't know whether they are devils or angels or what," he wrote, "but we all saw them, and my whole family saw the ship, and I don't want any more to do with them."

The day after Hamilton's heifer was stolen, Captain James Hooton of Homan, Arkansas, heard the sound of a steam engine and found, in a clearing, "a cylinder with pointed ends, lateral wheels, and horizontal blades over it." A man who wore dark glasses told Hooton that he was looking at ". . . the airship everyone had been seeing," and that it used compressed air for propulsion. Hooton saw the wheels spin as the craft rose and flew away. The week before, two farm workers in Springfield, Illinois, had been told that the strange craft they saw had flown from Quincy to Springfield in thirty minutes. At Farmersville, Texas, several persons saw an airship whose occupants, one said, could be heard singing "Nearer My God to Thee," as they handed out temperance tracts. (Texas seems to have been a focus of visitor activity at this time. There were thirty sightings of mysterious machines over the state during the period of April 15 to 28, 1897.) Sometimes the machines swept the ground with bright searchlights. One hooked Robert Hibbard of Sioux City, Iowa, with an anchor and dragged him 10 yards before he freed himself. The craft appeared "cigar-shaped with a dome," he said. "Like a ship with a roof and double canopy"; or "had four giant wings."

Witnesses finding machines on the ground being repaired, were given explanations of their operations that they could not follow. Frank Nichols, a farmer of Josserand, Texas, was informed that five "ponderous vessels of strange proportions" similar to that which landed in his cornfield, were being built in a small town in Iowa. The invention, his two visitors said, would "soon be given to the public. An immense company is now being formed and within the next year the machines will be in general use." There was usually something strange about the passengers who remained aboard. Some had long hair and others kept their faces averted, or hid when approached. Dogs barked at the machines and their occupants, and other animals acted disturbed. When repaired, the machines often flew off at great speed.

Now these descriptions of machines resemble drawings that had been appearing at the time in newspapers and magazines concerning an actual dirigible balloon that had been flown by some Frenchmen and other prospective flying machines that hadn't quite been invented.

In the 1950's: disks, cigars with exhausts, spools, spindles, and so on.

In the 1890's: dirigibles with wheels or propellers, sometimes with long wings.

In the 1600's: horses and coaches.

What does this suggest?

6

'h' and the End of the Ether

What is happening here? For the past two centuries science has been increasingly successful in separating that which *is* from that which *is not*. Laws have been found governing the motions of the universe, and the principle of continuity—that the laws that operate today and here also operated in the past and obtain in the farthest reaches of the cosmos—has yielded a wealth of knowledge. Many old beliefs have been demonstrated to be wrong. The evidence of rocks and fossils, for example, proved that Bishop Usher's famous calculation that the world began in the year 4004 B.C. was absurd.

As men discovered and mastered the chemical elements, creating dyes, fabrics, and medicines out of coal; as they increased their speed of travel and communications through controlled explosions and the marvels of electricity, knowledge and knowing became more and more thought of as *doing*. Certain kinds of knowledge—chemistry, physics, geology, biology—were real because they led to power, whether in the form of machines that turned without animal aid, the discovery of minerals and oil, the enrichment of crops, or the ability to kill more people from greater distances. Other kinds of knowledge, residing in the tales of old people in out-of-the-way places, memories of older times or queer things seen, were ignored to the extent that there was great surprise when some of their details were confirmed by the new kinds of knowledge.

In 1871, for example, the German, Henry Schliemann, found the city of Troy—at that time regarded only as a "legend"—by following the descriptions given in a 3,000-year-old epic poem, the *Iliad*. More recently, Israelis have used Biblical descriptions to find King Solomon's mines.

So we have two kinds of knowledge: "real" knowledge, the physical and biological sciences that give results; and "unreal" knowledge, which has long been ignored because it seems to have no practical application. There was another reason for ignoring "unreal" knowledge. The astonishing and rapid progress of the physical sciences made it seem likely that the laws and principles it discovered could be used to explain everything. Indeed, by the end of the nineteenth century, some savants were so taken with their achievements that they believed little else remained to be found out about the universe, and even ventured to feel sorry for their successors, who would be doing little more than mopping up after their predecessors. "Future discoveries," announced the great British scientist Lord Kelvin (1824-1907), "must be looked for in the sixth place of decimals."

To such a way of thinking, which has been shared by most educated people for the past hundred years, tales of little people who vanished were not only to be ignored because no use could be made of them, but had to be *untrue* because physical science could not explain them. This attitude, which has governed the official view of UFO's, and other unexplainable sightings, can be summed up as: "It can't be, therefore it isn't."

But if a scientist or educated layman had, in Lord Kelvin's time, to choose between physical science and fairies, this is no longer the case. The fact is that although most people are probably unaware of it, so-called physical science has changed a great deal in the past seventy-five years. The safe, explainable world of Kelvin's era was already being undermined just when he was expressing his foolish conceit.

Curiously, the investigations that destroyed the foundations of nineteenth-century science all were concerned with light. One of the puzzles of the nineteenth century was the nature of the substance that carried light waves. It had been discovered that light traveled at a certain speed, about 186,000 miles per second, and that it was a kind of wave. In a number of experiments since the time of Isaac Newton (1642-1727) light had been shown to do the sorts of things that waves—for instance, sound waves—do. Sound waves, depending on their frequencies (number of vibrations per second) can be made to reenforce or cancel each other out. Light could be made to do the same. The Englishman, James Clerk Maxwell (1831-1879), had further shown that light was electromagnetic in nature. Sound waves, nineteenth-century scientists knew, were carried by air, water, wood, metal, or some substance or *medium* that vibrated with them, transmitting the vibration from one place to another. They could not exist in a vacuum. Light waves, however, did seem to exist in the vacuum between the sun and the earth, for how else could sunlight reach here? Since there had to be a medium to carry the light waves as air carried sound waves, they believed something must exist in the vacuum that the best instruments available could not detect. This extremely tenuous medium was named the *ether*.

To detect the ether, the American, Alexander Michelson (1852-1931), devised a clever experiment. The earth went around the sun at 18 miles a second, about 1/10,000 the speed of light. As it circled the sun, Michelson reasoned, it must cut a swath through the ether. He built an apparatus that could detect extremely small changes in the direction or speed of light. It was sensitive enough to catch any bending of the light beam as, like a canoe trying to go straight across a rapidly flowing river, it crossed the ether; or to measure changes in its speed as it moved either with or against the "current." Michelson repeated this experiment several times in the 1880's, with ever more refined equipment, but could find no deviation, no matter what direction his light beam traveled in.

The experiment greatly upset many scientists, who decided that something was wrong with Michelson's apparatus. The alternative explanation, that there was no ether to carry light waves, was so painful to contemplate that even Michelson could not accept it.

About 1896, Max Planck, a young German, began wondering why substances changed color as they became hotter. This had been noticed for many hundreds of years, and, in fact, foundrymen determined the workability of iron by its hue. Scientists had measured the temperatures of iron, analyzed its light, and found that given colors (or frequencies) were precisely related to certain temperatures. What bothered Planck, however, was that according to known physical laws, this should not have happened. The accepted explanation for the broadcast of light by hot metal was that as more heat was applied, the heat energy increasingly agitated the particles of which the iron was made, and this vibration of the particles was observed by the eye as light. But if this were so, if all that the heat energy was doing was increasing the size of the vibrations, the *amplitude*, then the light should simply have become brighter without changing frequency—color. No matter how hard Planck tried, he could not, using existing physical principles, explain how an increase in energy led to a change in frequency rather than amplitude.

In 1900, after four years of thinking, Planck decided that the change of color could be explained if an assumption that scientists were making could be dropped. This assumption was that energy was *continuously* absorbed and emitted by the radiating body (iron). This was a reasonable, common-sense assumption (like the assumption that ether existed) based on the observation that everything in nature moved, flowed, or changed continuously. But the observed fact of frequency change could be explained only by assuming that energy was absorbed or emitted in little packages. The consequences of this idea were so astounding that Planck could not bring himself to believe that his was more than a theory. If changes took place by little spurts, rather than continuously, it meant that somewhere in the tiny invisible world all around us, there was a limit to what could happen. There was an event, named 'h' by Planck, than which there could be nothing smaller. At this limit, a particle did not move in a continuous path, *it jumped from one place to another.* One second it was *here.* Another second it was *there. Here* and *there* were disconnected. One would not, at this level, be able to say where a particle would be next. One could not say what would happen next.

The reasonable, predictable world in which A led to B, led to C, in which the motions of the moon could be computed to the second a century in advance seemed, if examined closely enough, to be built out of spontaneous, unpredictable jumping beans. The mind boggled at the thought.

Puzzles multiplied. More and more things were noticed that could not be explained within the system of knowledge that had worked so well for three hundred years. In France, the Curies found that a mysterious form of energy was given off by radium in defiance of another foundation-rock of science—that something could not come out of nothing.

It wasn't until 1905 that someone would make sense out of these weird observations. Instead of trying to save the old way of looking at things, Albert Einstein, a twenty-six-year-old clerk in the Swiss patent office, asked himself what sort of universe it would be if events really did have a lower limit and light could not vary in speed.

He was able to show that the littlest event, Planck's 'h,' did in fact exist, for it perfectly explained a mystery that was the opposite of the color changes that had bothered Planck. He used 'h' to explain why the energy of electrons, knocked from metal by impinging light, was related to the color of the light instead of its brightness. (An electron dislodged by blue light, for example, moved faster than one dislodged by red—the higher the frequency, the greater the velocity of the electron.)

When it came to constructing a system in which light speed remained invariable no matter what the direction or speed of the source, Einstein found himself describing a whole new universe.

If light speed was always the same, there could be no such thing as "real" motion at all. "Real" motion, based on common-sense ideas, implied a framework against which the motion was measured. As we go about earth, for example, our frame is the planet's surface and we compute speed and direction simply by referring to coordinates of latitude and longitude. At a simpler level, we judge the speed of an automobile in relation to the road on which it travels, and are always orienting ourselves by the landscape, by objects around us: houses, street signs, mountains, trees, and so on. The ether had been an extension of these ideas into the cosmos—a fluid, very tenuous, to be sure, that filled it inertly like a great jelly and that could act as a frame of reference to everything in it.

Einstein's universe had no such absolute frame of reference. The motion of earth could be computed relative to the sun, and that of the sun against other stars, but there was no single central place, no reference frame, against which one could determine the speed and direction of the sun or of anything, all by itself.

In such a universe, strange things had to happen to preserve the one invariant—the speed of light. As the velocity of a light source approached that of light itself, the source had to shorten in the direction of motion. Its mass had to increase, and even its time system had to change so that a second on a fast-moving body lasted longer than a second on a slower-moving body. Most momentous of all, energy and mass were interchangeable, for one result of these computations was the famous equation $e = mc^2$, which, incidentally, accounted for the mysterious energy of radium (infinitesimal amounts of matter were turning into energy).

It has taken a long time for these conceptions to sink into the popular culture, and indeed they are probably still not widely comprehended. But what they essentially mean—going from 'h' in the tiny world of particles to Einstein's universe of relativity—is that at both extremes of our common-sense everyday experience, the rules we base our earthly actions on do not apply. And as, in the years since 1905, we have explored the implications of these discoveries, we have come to perceive our habitation as increasingly curious.

The jumping, accidental world of particles has been incorporated into the orderly universe of laws of motion and of chemical reactions, by the idea of mathematical averaging. We now know that at our level of experience—we are very large in comparison with particles—we are customarily treating such large numbers of particles that we can deal with them only on a statistical basis. These statistics are our so-called "laws." In other words, if a single particle is unpredictable, a million will exhibit certain average kinds of behavior that are predictable in the aggregate, and a billion will be even more predictable. Similarly, at the speeds and energies we use in everyday life, far lower than the velocity of light, the Einstein effects are unnoticeable. But as we turn our eyes outward to the universe around us we find stars and conglomerations of stars radiating their mass out into space in different forms of energy, and the collapse of matter into "black holes," where time ends and everything disappears. We know, as our recent ancestors did not, that our orderly world is but a small special corner of the universe to which our eyes, ears, nervous system, and physical nature are adapted.

We also know that, as the UMMITES state, there is no reason to assume that the dimensions we operate in are the only ones. We perceive three spatial dimensions (length, breadth, thickness) and one of time, but this does not mean that no more exist any more than that our perceptions of light between the wavelengths of red and purple exclude the existence of infrared, ultraviolet, radio waves, and the entire enormous spectrum of electromagnetic radiation. And despite the fact that we are locked into perceiving time as flowing in one direction, there are no theoretical reasons why it cannot flow backwards (and in fact there are particle experiments that can be interpreted as examples of this).

Today's physicists see no reason not to postulate a universe with unlimited dimensions, of which we happen to be able to perceive only four. There could be an infinity of other universes, each with its own set of physical laws, of which we are unaware. Beings from some of these other universes might be able to enter and leave ours at will. They might exist in some alternative universe that contains some, or all, of our dimensions among theirs; or the laws of their universe might allow them to cross the boundary between universes, or they might have developed machines capable of crossing the boundary.

Such beings would in many ways be incomprehensible to us. For example, some writers have imagined a two-dimensional world whose inhabitants lived on the surface of a globe (see *Flatland*, by Edwin A. Abbott). They would be aware of right and left and backwards and forwards, but not of up and down. Assuming they were circular in shape, they would see each other as lines; or if they had the rectangular outlines of shoeboxes, they would appear to each other as lines of varying lengths, depending on the direction in which they were turned. Since they would have no conception of the shape of the sphere they inhabited, they would be puzzled by the way their friends would disappear over the horizon. Suppose one of us were to reach down, pick up a Flatman, and deposit him on a different spot on the sphere. He wouldn't have the foggiest notion as to how he got there. Suppose one of us landed on Flatworld on a ship? Whatever the shape of the craft, it would appear to the Flatman as a line. When we disembarked, we would look very much like one of them—like lines; but our appearance from "up" and departure to "up" as we took off, would be completely baffling. We would appear to have been there one moment, and gone the next.

7

What Are They?

◆ ◆

We are now in a position to speculate about the hobgoblins, brownies, elves, demons, fairies, sprites, and other beings that have been witnessed by mankind through the ages.

Let us review some of their characteristics. They appear and disappear mysteriously. They often give off strong emotional signals, either of friendliness or the opposite. Their time exists in a different sense from ours. They take things away but never leave anything that can be kept and examined. At times they foretell the future or issue dire warnings. They are invulnerable to our weapons and, presumably, to other effects of our environment. They are largely nocturnal, with large eyes adapted to dim light. Different forms exhibit different behavior patterns, from subhuman (bugs and bogys) to about our level (fairies), to superhuman (dwarfs whose compelling stares affect us as ours affect dogs and cats). Their habitations are mysteriously lit by glowing surfaces.

Their ability to appear and disappear mysteriously we can compare to our theoretical ability to do the same in Flatworld. In other words, it could be a result of their entering and leaving our universe from other dimensions of which we are unaware. This would also account for the difference in time sense. We would expect that time would flow in a different manner in other universes, either more swiftly or more slowly, or even backwards. If it flows backwards in the universe of the dwarfs, or at least of some of them, this would explain why most of the dwarfs seen hundreds of years ago had beards while those today usually do not. The clean-shaven dwarfs we see today could be beginning an investigation of earth that will end, say, a couple of thousands of years ago, when they are old and bearded. Moving backwards in our universe would also, of course, enable them to foretell our future, which they would have already seen.

The other-dimensionality could also account for the curious way in which Type 1 occupants blend into Type 2's, as they get taller. As beings, say, from a universe with six dimensions instead of four, what appears to us as their solid three-dimensional bodies would just be cross-sections of their true appearance, just as the lines that the Flatworlders would perceive as ourselves would be cross-sections of ourselves. Just as, to a Flatworlder, we would appear to vary in shape or length as we lowered ourselves—our legs would be two short lines, our belly one long line, our head one short line—so dwarfish Type 1's could become tall, more normal-looking Type 2's by rotating or moving through a dimension unknown to us. This would also account for reports of the shifting appearance of their "ships."

Their large eyes and sensitivity to light might indicate that light is of a lower intensity in their universe or that, perhaps, its physical laws being different, their eyes are sensitive to different parts of the electromagnetic spectrum. What appears to us as a glowing light from the surfaces of their dwellings, such as "saucers," might simply be the way matter of their universe affects our eyes. For all we know, we, or our trees, buildings, and so on, might appear to glow to them. Their other-dimensionality would also account for their invulnerability to our weapons, which could at most affect a tiny cross-section of their bodies. It is also possible that they are mere three-dimensional projections into our space, comparable to the two-dimensional images we project on motion-picture screens.

We do not, of course, have to assume that all these beings come from the same universe. Many Type 1's and 2's could very well be different appearances of the same beings, probably from the same place. The hairy little bugaboos might be pets of theirs, or animals, in which case their origin would be the same, or they might originate in a different universe. The formless, or only half-seen Type 4's could either have, again, a different home or be Type 1's that are only partly materialized or projected into our space.

What, then, are we to say about their stories of having come from Lanulos, Mars, or UMMO? What are we to say of their "flying machines"? Or of the complicated star chart they displayed to Betty Hill?

Dr. Jacques Vallee, the French astronomer, has made a list of the sightings of strange machines prior to August 1914. When they were described at all, their shape was given as that of a cigar. The thirty-third sighting, in August 1914, was of a spherical craft. The first saucer shape was reported three years later, in October, 1917, by James Boback of Youngstown, Pennsylvania, who saw it sitting in a field about 100 feet away from where he was walking along the railroad tracks. The next description of a strange machine came a generation later when, in September, 1943, an Argentinian driving between Rosario and Córdoba saw one on the ground about a quarter of a mile away. Thereafter, saucer became the prevailing shape, though it was occasionally intermixed with other shapes: cigars, tubes, and so on.

Now it is interesting that 1917, the first year that a "saucer" was seen, was a time when, due to the great spurt in technical development caused by the First World War, the shapes of airplanes were becoming widely known.

We had cigar-shaped craft with domes, paddlewheels, and various other devices appearing in the 1890's, when no one knew exactly what an aircraft was supposed to look like. Then, in 1917, when people did know, we had a saucer. It would appear that some sort of apparatus is used by the visitors and that this is what we see when we see a ship in the sky covered with a canopy, a cigar-shaped thing with wheels and wings, or a saucer, spindle, spool, or lantern. Obviously, they don't need this apparatus all the time. Sightings of aliens, without some sort of ship, may indicate:

a. *they don't always need this apparatus; or*
b. *some aliens have been left on earth for extended visits.*

The "ship," or whatever, that we see may be some sort of universe-penetrating machine or, perhaps, a glimpse into their universe through a temporarily open "door." In either case, since it is a multidimensional object, we have no way of telling what it really looks like, or is. As it rotates in its unknown dimensions it could change its aspect completely, getting bigger or smaller, longer or shorter, shifting color, or even disappearing.

It is well known that the human mind will try to make sense out of what it perceives. (This accounts for the "canals" on Mars, which the astronomer Percival Lowell constructed by mentally connecting the spots on the planet's surface that were at the limits of his vision.) So our minds, confronted with these strange appearances shading off into unknown dimensions, make of them machines that move in our skies in certain ways. A "saucer" could, for example, be growing smaller when an observer believes it is shooting up in the sky at great speed; and any of its maneuvers—stops, sharp right-angle turns—could be just our interpretations of movements in unknown dimensions.

Ball lightning could be either another class of occurrence entirely, and therefore completely unconnected with the visitors, or it could in some way tear the fabric of our universe, providing a means by which these creatures can enter.

When confronted in their Type 2 aspect by humans, the visitors often seem compelled to explain themselves. Their explanations are often, uncannily, exactly like the most recent theories that have been advanced to explain them. From the late 1940's to the 1960's, when the most accepted theory was that they were space travelers, they told Daniel Fry that they were a race of exiles from earth who had fled to Mars 30,000 years ago and had later taken up permanent residence in giant space ships. Later, when respectable scientists like Frank Drake and Carl Sagan, of Cornell, and I. S. Shklovskii, of Moscow University, began to speculate on the numbers of inhabited planets in the galaxy, along came Mr. Indrid Cold's stories of Lanulos in the galaxy of Ganymede and the UMMO reports, supported by details that could have been drawn from a university course in extraterrestrial life.

It would seem that our brains insist on seeing these manifestations, machines, open doors, or whatever as supporting the latest popular belief, whether religious, as at Knock, Ireland, or technological, and that these beings, aware of our speculations, suit their stories to them. We can only guess at why they do this. Perhaps it amuses them to play roles in our fantasies. The one thing we can be certain of is that they do not have a consistent wish to be inconspicuous. The Type 2's, those who appear most like us, spread these weird stories. The Type 1's are strange enough in appearance not to have to say anything to prove they are aliens.

It is also possible that another element enters into at least some of the Type 2's tales. That is, deliberate fabrication by certain groups on earth, for secret purposes. An example that raises suspicions of this sort is the story first told by Daniel Fry in 1954. The forty-five-year-old rocket technician wrote that on the night of July 4, 1950, while he was employed at White Sands, New Mexico, by Aerojet General Corporation, he went for a walk when the air-conditioner in his room broke down. A short distance from his quarters he saw, resting on the desert, a metallic-looking "oblate spheroid (football) about 30 feet in diameter and 16 feet high."

A voice addressed him in English, asking him if he wished to take a ride. When he agreed, he heard the sound of the "ship" filling with air and then, with a click, a small section of the hull moved back and sideways, leaving an oval-shaped doorway. Fry looked into "a room about nine feet deep and seven feet wide, with a floor about sixteen inches above the ground and the ceiling slightly over six feet above the floor.... The room contained four seats which looked like our modern body contour chairs, except ... somewhat small." The seats faced the opening in which Fry was standing, in two rows of two each. In the center of the rear wall he saw "a box or cabinet with a tube and lens which resembled a small motion picture projector," lacking visible spools or moving parts.

The beam from this machine spread over the door, which, the mysterious voice explained, had been rendered transparent. From then on, everything Fry saw was "through" this transparent door. What he saw was the surface of earth dropping away as the ship achieved altitude, and a panorama of the continent as they flew, with no sensation of motion of any kind, to hover over New York and return. The round trip took about thirty minutes, which means an average speed of about 8,000 miles per hour.

Subsequently, Fry had several messages from the visitors, who claimed they had recently come to earth and would not be fully adapted to our conditions until about 1954. The communicator, who introduced himself as Alan, was used to gravity only half as strong as earth's, as his ancestors had lived on Mars for many generations. They had left earth 30,000 years ago, when their civilization destroyed itself in a frightful war. After a long sojourn on Mars, during a period when it was more hospitable to human life than at present, they had decided to take up permanent residence in space, in large ships, some of which now orbited earth and from which they had dispatched the "oblate spheroid." They were coming, Alan said, to save mankind from another great disaster like that which had befallen them.

According to Fry's story, everything he saw was through the "transparent door." This could easily have been a projection on the door from the machine he noticed "in the center of the rear wall that ... resembled a motion picture projector." He did not see anyone, just heard voices, which could have come from hidden speakers. He also noted that he felt no sensation of motion except for a demonstration of weightlessness when they were approaching White Sands. This could have been simulated by allowing the room he was in to free fall in an elevator shaft. Fry's entire experience could have been arranged by earthlings using existing technology.

The "contactee experience of George Adamski, which was widely publicized in the 1950's and became the basis of a cult, could similarly have been faked. The "saucer" he saw land could, from his description, have been a large balloon fabricated into saucer shape, and the "Venusian" could have been an earthman or woman. In his book *Flying Saucers Have Landed*, Adamski even described the visits of various government personnel who, it would seem, set him up for his photography of "saucers" and "Venusians." (See pages 174-5, where he tells about the four men from the Point Loma Navy Electronics Laboratory, including one in naval-officer's uniform, who visited his café on Mount Palomar. On page 185 he is approached by two couples, complete strangers to him, the Baileys and the Williamsons, who take him to a desert rendezvous with the "Venusian," for which Williamson just happens to have with him some plaster of Paris to make castings of the visitor's footprints.)

The obvious source of these fake UFO experiences is the Central Intelligence Agency of the United States, founded in 1947. Dr. Leon Davidson, a computor scientist who worked for many years at government atomic installation research facilities and for the Atomic Energy Commission, is convinced that the CIA supported the publication of Adamski's and Fry's books and helped found many of the early saucer investigation groups.

As evidence of the CIA's involvement, Davidson points out that Admiral Hillenkoetter, the first CIA director, was active in NICAP (National Investigation Committee of Aerial Phenomena), and Davidson cites what happened when a Cincinnati businessman tried to sue Adamski as a charlatan. The businessman, Thomas Eickoff, had seen a UFO himself and was annoyed at the Air Force's insistence that all UFO reports were either fakes or based on ignorance. He decided to bring the issue to a head. In George Adamski's *Inside the Space Ships*, Eickhoff found the following statement: "I do have witnesses to one of my journeys in a space craft. Both are scientists who hold high positions. Once they are able to make a statement the picture will change overnight. However, the way things are nowadays, with everything classified as security, for the time being they must remain in the shadows. When they believe that they can release the substantiation they have without jeopardizing either the national defense or themselves, they have said that they will do so through the press...."

On July 7, 1952, the North American Newspaper Alliance sent out a story that the former mayor of a small East German city, who had escaped to the West, had seen a disk and two small men. The mayor, Oscar Link, who was accompanied by his eleven-year-old daughter, was reported to have said in a sworn statement that his "daughter called (his) attention to something shimmering through the trees in a small forest through which we were passing (on a motorcycle). We were . . . only about three miles from the border. . . . It was a disk about twenty-five feet across, resting on the ground in a clearing. . . . In the center was some sort of apparatus, a square contraption . . . which rose out of the top of the craft. . . . We saw two small figures, like tiny human beings, about three and one-half feet tall. They were wearing what appeared to be shiny, one-piece garments, aluminum or silver in color. . . . The creatures hastily entered the craft through a porthole in the top . . . the upperworks began to retract into the dome and simultaneously the object started to rise slowly off the ground. . . . It rose to about one hundred feet, hovered, and sped away."

Some people believe this story, like a number of other UFO stories, was invented by the CIA.

As this was not a personal opinion as to what Adamski thought he had seen, but a statement of fact citing witnesses, Eickhoff reasoned that it could be tested in court and that the scientists mentioned by Adamski would have to be produced. If they testified in the manner outlined by Adamski, the case for the UFO's would be proved and the Air Force and other government agencies would no longer be able to deride UFO reports. On the other hand, if the scientists did not testify, Adamski would be convicted of mail fraud, for Eickhoff had gone to the trouble of procuring a copy of the book advertised by mail order.

After several weeks of checking with various Washington agencies and receiving several requests to hold off the suit, Eickhoff's attorney got a letter from Alan Dulles, director of the CIA, admitting that Eickhoff did have a case for mail fraud. Dulles added, however, that if necessary he would use a court injunction to prevent anyone from testifying in court on the Adamski book because "maximum security exists concerning the subject of UFO's." As a result of this message, Eickhoff dropped the case.

The CIA has several motives for being involved with "saucers." Some of the strange things seen in the skies by trained pilots, particularly when also manifested on radar, may be secret electronic measures designed to confuse enemy aircraft in case of war. The reports of "contactees," like Fry and Adamski, could be CIA experiments in psychological warfare. The "messages" could be created to further certain United States policies—for example, the dire warnings about atomic warfare and atomic testing furthered efforts to achieve a test-ban treaty.

The UMMO papers have all the earmarks of a similar, if more elaborate, CIA hoax, perhaps designed to see how certain groups in other countries can be manipulated.

We cannot, therefore, ignore the possibility that in addition to hobgoblins, elves, fairies, and demons from other universes, we may also be seeing "aliens" or "messages" produced by the human "spooks" of the CIA or other intelligence agencies.

All we can do is keep our eyes and ears open for strange visitors and their manifestations, and understand in our hearts that the universe is stranger than we think. It is a safe guess that it shall be many years before we capture a gnome or any evidence of his existence. By then, perhaps, we shall have learned to penetrate the other mansions of the cosmos.

Notes

Chapter 1.

Flying Saucer Review
   Vol. 18, No. 5, pp. 11–15.
   Vol. 19, No. 1, pp. 19–21.
   Vol. 20, No. 4, pp. 12–16.
   Vol. 20, No. 5, pp. 6–7, 10–11.
   Vol. 20, No. 6, pp. 13, 23.
   Vol. 21, No. 1, p. 20.
   Vol. 21, No. 2, p. 13.
   Vol. 21, No. 3–4, p. 3.
J. A. Keel, *The Mothman Prophecies*, pp. 51–55.
Jacques Vallee, *Passport to Magonia*, pp. 195, 196, 132–135, 245, 247, 303.
Daniel W. Fry, *The White Sands Incident*.
C. Bowen, ed., *The Humanoids*, 179, 200–238, 246–247.
J. G. Fuller, *Interrupted Journey*.
R. & J. Blum, *Beyond Earth: Man's Contact With UFO's*, pp. 109–118.
Le Figaro, September 13, 1954.
"Document 96", p. 117.

Chapter 2.

Flying Saucer Review, Vol. 20, No. 5, p. 16.

Chapter 3.

C. Sagan and T. Page, eds., *UFO's, A Scientific Debate*, pp. xxi, xxii, xxvii, xxix.
Cleveland *Plain Dealer*, October 20, 1973.
"Proceedings, Eastern UFO Symposium," pp. 14–15.
Blue Book Special Report, No. 14, pp. 78–90.
P. J. Klass, *UFO's Identified*, pp. 76, 77.
Dr. E. U. Condon, *Scientific Study of Unidentified Flying Objects*, pp. 248–255.

Chapter 4.

"2nd Midwest UFO Conference," pp. 23–30.
Mothman Prophecies, pp. 51–61.
Flying Saucer Review, Vol. 19, No. 3, pp. 19–22.
Humanoids, p. 96.

Chapter 5.

K. M. Briggs, *The Fairies in Tradition and Literature*, pp. 133, 146.
J. A. Hynek, *The UFO Experience*, p. 130.
J. G. Fuller, *Incident at Exeter*.
UFO's Identified, p. 109.
National Enquirer, September 26, 1976, p. 3.

Chapter 7.

Magonia, pp. 188, 190.
D. Leslie and G. Adamski, *Flying Saucers Have Landed*.
Leon Davidson, *Flying Saucers*.
D. E. Keyhoe, *Flying Saucer, Top Secret*.

Bibliography

Blum, R. and J., *Beyond Earth: Man's Contact With UFO's.* New York: Bantam Books, 1974.

Bowen, C., ed., *The Humanoids.* Chicago: Henry Regenery, 1969.

Briggs, K. M., *The Fairies in Tradition and Literature.* London: Routledge & Kegan Paul, 1967.

Condon, Dr. E. U., *Scientific Study of Unidentified Flying Objects.* New York: Bantam Books, 1969.

Davidson, Leon, *Flying Saucers: An Analysis of the Airforce Project Bluebook Report No. 14,* 2nd. rev. ed. Clarksburg: Best Books, 1967.

Edwards, G., *Hobgoblin and Sweet Puck.* London: Geoffrey Bles, 1974.

Fry, Daniel W., *The White Sands Incident.* Merlin: Best Books, 1964.

Fuller, J. G., *Incident at Exeter.* New York: G. P. Putnam, 1967.

———*Interrupted Journey.* New York: Berkeley Pub., 1974.

Funk and Wagnall's Standard Dictionary of Folklore, Mythology and Legend. New York: Funk and Wagnalls, 1950.

Hynek, J. A., *The UFO Experience.* Chicago: Henry Regenery, 1972.

Keel, J. A. *The Mothman Prophecies,* New York: Saturday Review Press, 1975.

Keyhoe, D. E., *Flying Saucer, Top Secret.* New York: Holt, 1959.

Kirk, R., *The Secret Commonwealth of Elves, Fauns and Fairies,* with foreword by A. Lang. London: D. Nutt, 1893.

Klass, P. J., *UFO's Identified.* New York: Random House, 1968.

Leslie, D., and G. Adamski, *Flying Saucers Have Landed.* New York: British Book Center, 1953.

Lorenzen, C., *Flying Saucer Occupants.* New York: Signet, 1966.

Proceedings, Eastern UFO Symposium, Jan. 23, 1971. Tucson: Aerial Phenomenon Research Organization (APRO), 1971.

Sagan, C., and T. Page, eds., *UFO's, A Scientific Debate.* Ithaca: Cornell University Press, 1972.

2nd Midwest UFO Conference, June 12, 1971. Midwest UFO Network (MUFON), 1971.

Vallee, Jacques, *Passport to Magonia.* Chicago: Henry Regnery, 1969.

Periodicals

Dublin Review, p. 324, 1915.

Flying Saucer Review, 1969 to date.

Occult Review, pp. 327–336, 1916.

Index

Abbott, Edwin A., 82
Adamski, George, 88
Aerojet General Corp., 86
Alabama, 42
Alamo, Domingo, 74
Alien, Type 1, 53
Alien, Type 2, 54
Alien, Type 3, 57
Alien, Type 4, 57
APRO, 51
Argentina, 31
Arkansas, 76
Australia, 30

Baileys, 88
Ball lightning, 71
Batti, 72
Belgium, 14
Bello, Dr. Fernando, 74
black hole, 81
Boback, James, 85
bogys, 66
Brazil, 11, 20, 27
Briggs, Katherine, 67
brownies, 65
bugs, 66
Butterfield, William, 68

California, 23, 88
Canada, 26
CIA, 88
Cold, Indrid, 17, 86
Conrad, Peter, 43
Coyne, Capt. Lawrence J., 43
Creighton, Gordon, 31

da Silva, José Antonio, 11
Davidson, Dr. Leon, 88
Derenberger, Woodrow, 17
DeWilde, Marius, 28
dimensions, 82
Drake, Frank, 86
Dulles, Allen, 90
dwarfs, 66

East Germany, 31, 89
Eickhoff, Thomas, 88

Einstein, Albert, 80
electromagnetism, 76
electronic countermeasures, 90
elves, 65
England, 49, 68
ether, 79

fairies, 65
fireball, 72
Flammarion, Camille, 70
Flatland, 82
flying saucer, 39, 72, 84, 90
France, 20, 28, 31, 32
Fry, Daniel, 19, 86
Fuller, John, 72

Ganymede, 17
Gemini III, 43
General Mills Aeronautical Research
   Laboratory, 40
Gill, Rev. William B., 8
gnomes, 65
Gonzales, Gustav, 27
Grand Canary Islands, 73

'h,' 80
Hamilton, Alexander, 75
Hewes, Hayden C., 52
Hibbard, Robert, 76
Higdon, Carl, 15
High-tension power line, 72
Hill, Barney, 20
Hillenkoetter, Admiral, 88
hobgoblins, 65
Hooton, Captain James, 76
Hynek, Alan, 70

Illinois, 41, 76
Indiana, 40
Iowa, 38, 70, 76
Ireland, 19
Isle of Man, 67
Italy, 8, 10, 72
Ivorde, M., 14

Kansas, 75
Kentucky, 26, 51

Kirk, Robert, 65
Klass, Philip J., 71
Korea, 48
kugelblitz, 71

landing circles, 70
Lanulos, 17
light, 76
Link, Oscar, 89
Lorenzen, Coral, 51
Lotti, Rosa, 9
Lowell, Percival, 85
Lubbock lights, 69

McLoughlin, Mary, 19
Mars, 85, 86
Masse, Maurice, 23
Maxwell, James Clerk, 76
Menzel, Donald, 69
Michelson, Abraham, 79
MUFON, 52

Nebraska, 24
Newfoundland, 72
New Guinea, 8
New Hampshire, 20, 72
New Mexico, 19, 39
Newton, Isaac, 78
Nichols, Frank, 76
Northwestern University, 70
Novoa, Villagrassa, 31

Ohio, 43
Oklahoma, 64
Oregon, 71

Padron, Dr. Francisco, 73
Pennsylvania, 85
Phillips, Ted, Jr., 69
Planck, Max, 79

Point Loma Navy Electronics Laboratory, 88
Ponce, José, 27
Portugal, 57
Project Blue Book #14, 45

radar, 48, 90
relativity, 81
Ribera, Antonio, 31

Sagan, Carl, 86
Schirmer, Herbert, 24
Scotland, 67, 68
Shklovskii, I. S., 86
South Dakota, 40
SPADATS, 49
Spain, 57

Texas, 64, 76
Thomas, Link, 75
thunderstorm, 72
tornado, 72
Trent, Paul, 71

UFO landings, 69
U.S. Air Force, 14, 15, 88
UMMO, 31, 90
Usher, Bishop, 77

Valle, Dr. Jacques, 84
Venezuela, 27
Venusian, 88
Villas Boas, Antonio, 20

Wales, 67, 68
West Virginia, 17
Williamsons, 88
Will-o-the-Wisp, 66
Wolf 424, 33, 67
Wyoming, 15